Born Illiterate

Gender and Representation in Gadda's *Pasticciaccio*

Born Illiterate
Gender and Representation in
Gadda's *Pasticciaccio*

Rodica Diaconescu-Blumenfeld

Published by
Troubador Publishing Ltd
12 Manor Walk, Coventry Road
Market Harborough
Leics LE16 7BP, UK
Tel: (+44) 1858 469898
Fax: (+44) 1858 431649
Email: troubador@compuserve.com

in association with

 Hull Italian Texts
Department of Italian
University of Hull
Hull HU6 7RX
Email: a.d.thompson@selc.hull.ac.uk

Series Editor
Professor A. D. Thompson
University of Hull, UK

ISBN 1 899293 61 2

Cover design: Pen, ink and watercolour adaptation by Doug Thompson of the original 1957 cover to Gadda's *Pasticciaccio*.

Typesetting: Troubador Publishing Ltd, Market Harborough, UK
Printed and bound by Selwood Printing Ltd, UK

Contents

Acknowledgements

I want to offer my profound thanks to Olga Ragusa, Michael Riffaterre, Luciano Rebay, Robert Dombroski, Doug Thompson, William Weaver, Victor and Floritza Diaconescu, Bruno Blumenfeld, Elisabeth Ladenson and especially to Lucia Lermond. My thanks also to Garzanti Editore for permission to reproduce text from the *Pasticciaccio*, and finally to George Braziller, Inc. for permission to reproduce the texts of Gadda in translation.

HULL ITALIAN TEXTS

I Introduction

Gender, Power, Writing

Zamira, decaying madam of Carlo Emilio Gadda's *Quer pasticciaccio brutto de via Merulana*,[1] tells the peasant who declares woman "a great mystery", "un gran mistero" (242), that woman is a mystery you can understand, if you have a little imagination, "un mistero che se capisce subbito, basta avecce la fantasia", "a mystery immediately understood, if you have enough imagination[2] for it". The "great" mystery requires merely sufficient imagination. Against "grande", she sets "basta". Against "great", she sets "sufficient". The mystery of woman will be immediately understood, by a man with enough imagination. Immediately you will have "enough", because it does not take a "great" deal of imagination. "You'll catch on quick". A little is enough.

Does the old whore disparagingly declare that women only want a little something, a little something from men, that if you understand this little something about them, the little something they want, the mystery becomes transparent? Or does she rather suggest that really there is not so very much difference between women and men, that they are really more alike than not, that to see this alikeness across a bit of difference would only take a little, the little bit of imagination that men have always lacked?

Gadda's novel suggests that he has this little bit of imagination, of "fantasia". Like the author protagonist of his *Cognizione del dolore* who exclaims, "A novel! With female characters!", Gadda will use his "experience of the human psyche", "also his own", to write of them (1969: 207).[3]

To read the *Pasticciaccio* then, Gadda's epistemological murder mystery, is to be drawn into reflection upon female, upon male, upon the difference between them, upon the writing of female, male, difference, upon writing.

The novel articulates a series of intermeshing questions. What does it mean to write male and female characters? What is the difference between male and female? What does it mean to write? What does representation involve, linguistically, ontologically, morally? Representation is also an issue of difference, played out by Gadda as a tension of difference between two terms. Thus the problematic of gender and that of representation merge in his novel.[4]

In the *Pasticciaccio*, certain of the female characters become locus of a special function, the symbolization of Gadda's own literary enterprise as at once sadism and portrayal. They become privileged bearers of the dimension of the novel that is Gadda's meditation on the nature of representation.[5] A classic objectification/mystification of Woman takes its narrative place in a differential calculus of gender, wherein Gadda sorts difference itself. This is not to claim that gender is the only axis of polarization present in the *Pasticciaccio* offering access to Gadda's theorization of writing. There are multiple others, as life/death, time/space, seeing/hearing, remembering/ forgetting, some of which intersect the gender system.

Still, gender remains a peculiarly powerful field of play. Again and again, in his literary and critical writings, Gadda evinces special concern with this theme:[6] men and women are different; men and women are not different; men and women are only a little different. What is this little difference? Finally, what is difference? The *Pasticciaccio* shows that to ask about gender is to ask about difference.

Gadda's gender reversals, slippages, ambiguities, doubles, his whole set of twists and turns, serve to thematize the stylistic flux of the *Pasticciaccio* as a whole, the flux through which he seeks to escape the necessarily totalizing control of his own authorial enterprise. Whether in *verismo* or expressionism, the mimesis of the literary work conceives beings whose existence the author controls absolutely. He is their fate. He is their executor, their executioner. Certainly, in murder mysteries, countless victims have met horrible deaths, one might say, gratuitous deaths, since the victims' authors need not have engendered or destroyed them. What is this species of phantom cruelty, of cruelty to phantoms? Can the act of representation itself be understood as a form of sadism? More, can self-reflexivity in writing issue in a moral crisis that an author struggles to inscribe, finally to fall into extratextual defeat, the silence outside the text, marking not its closure, but the author's exhaustion?[7]

The Plot of the *Pasticciaccio*

The narrative elaboration of *Quer pasticciaccio brutto de via Merulana* renders impossible an absolute schematization of levels of plot. What is important cannot finally be sorted from what is unimportant for the configuration of the novel. My summary, then, sketches the outline of the story for the purpose of providing a context for those characters and events analyzed in this study.

Gadda has set his work in the year 1927, the Fascist dictatorship of Mussolini in full bloom. Philosophizing police detective Francesco Ingravallo (called also Don Ciccio), thirty-five years old, is introduced as the novel's protagonist. The *Pasticciaccio*'s plot will center about Ingravallo's investigation of two crimes committed at the same address on the via Merulana, the theft of the Countess Menegazzi's jewels and the murder of Liliana Balducci, with whose household Ingravallo is on friendly terms.

Ingravallo visits the Balducci home, admires the beautiful and refined Liliana, and speculates about her secret sorrow. The household is childless, but a progression of 'nieces' have sequentially been adopted, among them the calculating Ines and the wild, insolent Virginia. Likewise, a progression of earthy and attractive maids have served the Balduccis, the present being the vital Assunta. The party is joined by Giuliano Valdarena, a handsome young cousin of Liliana's, to whom Ingravallo takes an immediate dislike.

When an intruder relieves the countess of her jewels (among which a fabulous topaz ring), Ingravallo questions the various tenants of 219 via Merulana. Several important clues emerge: a torn tram ticket showing part of a place name, the greenish scarf described as worn by the thief, and the young "delivery boy" who appears to have served as lookout. Civil servant Commendatore Angeloni, whose traffic with delivery boys bearing elegant comestibles brings him under suspicion, is brought in for further questioning, as he will be again in the course of the story.

The brutal murder of Liliana follows shortly thereafter. Ingravallo's investigation of the crime not only seeks to discover her murderer, but also to reveal and understand the motivations of his adored lady.

Ingravallo questions Liliana's cousin, who is found at the scene of the crime, her husband Remo, and Don Lorenzo Corpi, her confessor.

Involved in the investigations are both police and carabinieri. Notable among the latter are the motor-cycle riding Brigadiere Pestalozzi and his virile superior Maresciallo Santarella.

The carabinieri's search for the green scarf leads to the country tavern of Madame Zamira, dyeress, procuress, fortune-teller, whose establishment is graced by its own young seamstress/'nieces.' Brought in to be dyed, the scarf is ultimately traced to one Enea Retalli.

Dottor Fumi, Ingravallo's superior, having connected the reconstructed name from the tram ticket with the origin of a young woman booked on suspicion of prostitution and theft, calls her in for questioning. Subjected to several rounds of interrogation, Ines Cionini, a former employee of Zamira's, recounts her seduction and betrayal by Diomede Lanciani, himself a tutee of the country madam. Ines speaks of her betrayer with pride. An electrician, he had even done a job for a countess (obviously La Menegazzi). But it is the chance word that Ines lets fall, at the very end of the interviews, that gives the investigators the clue that they need, by leading them to Diomede's brother Ascanio, the "delivery boy", now selling roast pork in the market.

On his way to further official queries at the workshop-tavern of Zamira, Pestalozzi falls into a reverie about his strange dream of the preceding night, a dream in which a topaz prominently figures. This topaz, he immediately discovers upon the hand of Zamira's young seamstress Lavinia Mattonari. Pestalozzi takes Lavinia into custody, and, commandeering a buggy with driver, forces Lavinia to take him to the railroad crossing home of her cousin Camilla Mattonari. There the hidden jewels, left with Camilla by Enea Retalli, are recovered. Having informed Camilla's uncle by telephone that the post will be left unattended, the carabinieri send the girls off to be questioned.

Meanwhile, Ingravallo, at last given access to the official car, is able to travel to the countryside to question the Balduccis' maid Assunta, who had left prior to the murder to nurse her dying father. On Ingravallo's confrontation with Assunta the novel ends.

Writing about Gadda

Writing about Carlo Emilio Gadda presents methodological difficulties. One of them, in no way minor, is that of addressing in English a highly complex and idiosyncratic Italian combining slang, dialect, technical terminology, and etymological puns. William Weaver's translations of Gadda's two novels are very good, yet often one finds that the spheres of connotations of Italian and English expressions are sometimes approximate, if they do not actually differ. Thus, as always in the field of translation, a literal rendering is sometimes the best, at other times incomprehensible. Choices have to be made, since explanations (much as they may be needed) are precluded. Writing about Gadda, however, and not *translating* him, is a medium that offers the possibility of circumscribing the intransitivity of idiom.

The first purpose of this study is to give access to the *Pasticciaccio*, but this means generating a technique of articulating and ordering the diverse elements of the novel that yet displays their complex mesh.

Metaphors for my critical method can be drawn from Gadda's novel. This study is a look at the 'knot' of the *Pasticciaccio* from the inside, an inside look at a 'knot' or 'tangle' that cannot be untied. This study lays out a hand of cards to tell a fortune, describing the affinities and influences of the various cards, as the gypsy Zamira does.

Hence, I examine certain characters, incidents, images, first in one context, then in another, iterating the character, incident, image, through narrative and stylistic amplifications. The exposition, then, cannot be perfectly linear. Moreover, my reader will need repetition to stay in control of the interconnections.

The attempt to reconstitute analytically the novel as vortex of permutations cannot be absolutely achieved. It needs an instrument to prise apart the dimensions before reforming them into the space of the novel. I have made gender my instrument, the differential instrument enabling me to reveal the play of unity and difference in Gadda's text.

* * *

At present few book-length studies of Gadda exist in English, though a number of articles in journals of Italian Studies show an increased interest in his work.[8]

In Italy, Gadda has always had a following among the literary intelligentsia, and such seminal studies of Gadda as those of Contini, Guglielmi, Segre, Pasolini, Roscioni, remain basic to the critical canon. In recent years a considerable number of books on Gadda have appeared with concerns related to those of my study: style, representation, woman.

Gadda's narrative technique positions him at a point of tension for contemporary critical theory, really the point at which various postmodernisms confront more classical formulations of literary function. Reading *Quer pasticciaccio brutto de via Merulana* becomes an exercise in the theorization of closure, for reading it demands reflection upon meaning and indeterminacy. Hence, this study, through interpretation of the *Pasticciaccio*, engages in an exploration of critical categories.

This study exists at the intersection of Italian Literary Studies, Critical Theory, and Feminism. I write for scholars of Gadda and of Italian literature generally, for academics working in other areas of literature and literary theory, and for feminists concerned with the analysis of gender. My purpose is to clarify interpretation of the novel, to articulate problems of theory implicit in it, and, ultimately, to introduce a larger public to the prolific pleasures of this remarkable text.

Narrative Proliferation: Style Against Plot

Gadda was born in Milan in 1893 and died in Rome in 1973. By training, he was an engineer. The beginnings of his career as writer are connected to the literary magazine *Solaria*, in the 1920s, where many of his contemporaries published what was called "prosa d'arte", a writing practice not unrelated to hermeticism. Privileging style over realist mimesis, this current was fueled (as were the works of some better known European writers, such as Joyce and Proust) by introspection, lyricism, aestheticism, gaining for itself the reputation of moral indifference. In Gadda, style works against the linear development of plot, but, as I will argue, this itself is a dimension of the permeation of his works by ethics.

In his later years, Gadda was claimed by the Italian new avantgarde (the *Gruppo 63*) as a precursor, and was labeled as an experimentalist.[10] Soon, however, his work was seen not as a part of any current, but standing on its own, in isolation and inimitability. That Gadda represents the "spirit of a nation", or of a time, is undeniable: Contini identified a "Gadda function" in Italian literature, going back to the *maccheronea* of Teofilo Folengo in the sixteenth century. The late nineteenth-century Lombard *scapigliati*, and Gadda's beloved poet of plebeian Rome, Giuseppe Gioachino Belli, belong to the same kind of subversive, satirical literature whose apogee is found in Gadda.

In the *Pasticciaccio*, Gadda, "supremo maccaronico", as Contini calls him (1970: 581), 'macaronizes' a classic genre, the detective story. A genre defined above all by plot, Gadda explodes it through radical proliferation. The elements of the story – characters, objects, words – take off to become para-narratives, twisting and turning, inscribing themselves one within the other.

The usual detective story moves toward a solution that corresponds to the resolution or closure of the narrative. The detective/the reader comes to know: the mystery is over.[11] In counterdistinction, Gadda's *Pasticciaccio* is, as Olga Ragusa denominates it, a detective novel without solution (139). *Quer pasticciaccio brutto de via Merulana* displays the epistemological problematic of the detective novel through the process of subverting the plot. And "la femme" for whom it is necessary to search figures here also at the matrix of style as incompletion – woman as greatest mystery, the absolute adventure of (male) cognition. Gadda's treatment of women in the *Pasticciaccio* shows both continuities and discontinuities with this gendered epistemology.

The interrelations of knowledge, closure, gender, a constellation that structures my own study, have been variously formulated by Gadda's critics.[12]

* * *

Alba Andreini is responsible for the coming to light of a text written by Gadda after the publication of the *Pasticciaccio*, the 1957 film script *Palazzo degli ori*. Her studies – "Storia interna del *Pasticciaccio*" [Internal Story of the *Pasticciaccio*] and "Codicillo:*Il palazzo degli ori*" [Appendix: The Palace of Gold] (79–152) – of the two texts, together with that of the five chapters published from 1946 to 1947 in *Letteratura*, constitute the case-history of the *Pasticciaccio*. Andreini interrelates closure and the feminine, wherein she sees Gadda's search for "the truer *quid*" behind the "kaleidoscopic appearance" of reality through his use of ambiguity, uncertainty and mystery (both as narrative techniques and plot elements) (131).

Lucilla Sergiacomo, with awareness of contemporary feminist categories and with a rare clarity of style, looks at Gadda's entire narrative opus and proposes a typology of his women based on the classical opposition angel/demon: bestial woman, vital woman, transgressive mother. Though operative to a certain extent, this typology does not exhaust the characters in Gadda, or rather, reduces many of the women of the *Pasticciaccio* – from Zamira to Countess Menegazzi, to Ines and most of the other maids/nieces/apprentices – to pure negativity, unknowable and contemptible. This, Sergiacomo affirms, is a notion inherited by Gadda from traditional western culture (83), redeemed by his attempt to depict the position of woman in society with the anthropologist's or sociologist's understanding (85). But, though her interpretation of Gadda's misogyny as critique of dominant ideology is a very fine idea, she seems unaware of Gadda's continuous subversion of his own assumptions, the feature most emphasized by my own analysis.

More theoretically elaborated than Sergiacomo's study, is Maurizio de Benedictis' book, *La piega nera. Groviglio stilistico ed enigma femminile in C. E. Gadda* [The Black Fold: Stylistic Tangle and the Enigma of Femininity in C. E. Gadda]. Its very title evinces the identity of a central concern of this author with mine: the impossibility of epistemic closure in relation to woman. Locating in Gadda the Aristotelian distinction between form and matter, traditionally assimilated to the opposition male/female, De Benedictis employs it to construct his reading of cognition and the inexhaustible matrices of female being.

De Benedictis' development of this dynamic is very close to my work on sublimation and displacement (epistemic and erotic), but I believe he has failed (through his own misogyny, most evident in his emphatic reading of penis-envy, 167–68, n.89) to find in Gadda the critique of woman's mystification, the struggle to transcend it and to understand the sameness of men and women as human.

His strange metaphor for female genitalia is, in this context, particularly suggestive. He asserts that for Gadda, female organization (the expression is Gadda's, "l'organizzazione femminile") is "that which stands before the subject" and which the subject (male consciousness) will fail "to know, to penetrate exhaustively" (9), just as, at the end of the *Pasticciaccio*, the black vertical fold in Assunta's forehead blocks Ingravallo's attempt to break her down. "Such a 'fold,' recurring in other texts, with all its anatomical implications", De Benedictis writes, "is the tip of the iceberg of an inextricable tangle"! A peculiar and telling phrase, in that the critic is describing the *freezing* of the *male* (i.e., his castration) when confronted by the female genitalia.

* * *

The literature on Carlo Emilio Gadda has consistently laid great emphasis upon Gadda's theory of cognition, and upon those textual strategies by which it is expressed or embodied. Thus, Giorgio Patrizi writes that Gadda's act of writing structures itself not only as an enterprise of expression, but also as "cognitive process... which tests in its course all the possibilities... of reality" (222). Through philosophy, psychology, the study of myth, linguistics and theories of narrative, a converging point of research on Gadda is his epistemology. This special interest is reinforced by Gadda's theoretical writing, in which he presents a developed philosophy of knowledge and representation (in particular, his *Meditazione milanese*).

Because Gadda's major works, *La cognizione del dolore*, and *Quer pasticciaccio brutto de via Merulana*, remain unfinished, the issue of closure is often linked by interpreters to his epistemology, one that postulates a continuously self-deforming reality and the distortion operated by the act of cognition. Gadda writes, "the *datum* or reality is a pause in the process of deformation in action, a deformation that operates as correction... or as introduction of relations continuously different" (1974: I,56).

Thus, Jacqueline Risset argues that "Gadda's text can only be approached through the problematic of... incompletion". She relates the impossibility of total representation to Gadda's pluralistic theory of knowledge and to the necessary changes in narrative style: the text's avoidance of its "point of origin" is complemented by the desire to locate "the point that impedes closure". Thus the lack of completion is seen as a logical consequence of the refusal of teleology (950–51).

Gian Carlo Roscioni, on the other hand, proves, through textual analysis and the close reading of the author's self-critical writings (92), that to connect the actual "incompiutezza" (incompleteness) of Gadda's novels to his theory of "indeterminacy deriving from the impossible closure of systems" (1974: XIV, 62), is not legitimate.

That Gadda's philosophy and his narrative practice are related is incontrovertible. He did fight (as he wrote that matter does) against the "intolerable tyranny of finality" (1974: 196). But the unfinished work cannot be simply identified with an "opera aperta", which, no less than the closed, finds its character in closure.

Robert S. Dombroski sees incompletion as tied with the Bergsonian negation of an *a priori* philosophy, and in the practice of ending his texts abruptly, Gadda's "ethical mission to eradicate the falsity of the external world", grounded in myths of totality and purpose (1974: 56). In the new-wave context of the "arbitrariness of mimesis" (1974: 50f), Gadda, Dombroski writes, "brings literary subjectivism to a point where the novel is no longer possible" (1974: 126f). Gadda's "ethical mission" is indeed deeply embedded in his choice of style, and Dombroski sees in Gadda's use of dialects a "defense against oppression, be it linguistic or political" (1974: 58).

On the contrary, Pier Paolo Pasolini, one of Gadda's most astute critics (though he wrote little on him), develops a theory of Gadda as passive, non-militant, though prey to social and moral angst. He bases his interpretation on an analysis of the tenses used in the *Pasticciaccio*. Comparing Gadda with Manzoni, Pasolini points out Gadda's refusal of historical and logical perfect tenses, and his predilection for the pluperfect – an operation which equalizes the marginal and the essential in the story.

Gadda's experimentalism can be viewed from the perspective of his refusal of traditional techniques of closure. The tension with closure generates an anti-linear narrative form. The story refuses itself and proliferates as epistemic depth.[13]

Roscioni notes that "the concept of *pasticcio* (pastiche, mess) is related and often coincides with that of *groviglio* (tangle)". "The *pasticcio* of the crime is rendered through the linguistic *pasticcio*" (83), which in turn tends to identify itself with the notion of a complicated but organic structure, the idea of an order in which *tout se tient* (75). This would seem to support an essential monism in Gadda, but if a monist, how does Gadda conceive of difference in relation to unity? Is there rather for him an irreducible plurality of nontotalizable elements? Does his tension with closure result from this plurality, or from a totality that blocks the narrative, forcing it back on itself, back into its own complexity?

Roscioni believes that Leibnizian categories are at work in Gadda, but they are deformed, deharmonized. Risset, taking up this thesis, is very good in her treatment of the transformation: "The walls of the monad have become porous, the substantives empty themselves in favour of terms of qualification, which indicate the object's position in the universe. We have, in short, a monadology without monads, and this is perhaps precisely the operation of writing" (261). Leibniz' monad contains the totality of its predicates, but in Gadda they are bled out into the tangle, the knot. Gadda's "pause", the paradox of the impossible *datum*, articulates a knot of predicates.

Thus, I would say that it is rather as elements of style that Leibnizian categories are appropriated by Gadda's narrative technique. Because, for all the evocative force of Roscioni's title, *La disarmonia prestabilita* (The Preestablished Disharmony, based on Leibniz's "preestablished harmony"), Gadda is neither Leibnizian nor counter-Leibnizian. It is possible to interpret Gadda in terms of Leibniz, as Risset does, but not, I think, correct to read him in tension with Leibniz. Gadda's use of philosophical concepts is indistinguishable from his use of images. The philosophical themes do not organize his writing, do not unify it, anymore than the proliferating metaphors of everyday objects. Philosophical concepts have no priority here. Gadda uses the Leibnizian "compossibility" and makes a Leibniz joke about Ingravallo's landlady's pink robe, which, touching the ground behind her, "withdraws" her steps "one after the other, from the perception of third parties; and there remained in the hall, like a belated trail, the very idea of continuity in the infinitesimal sense of the term" (364/260). The continuum is a specifically Leibnizian problematic and Leibniz employs the concept of the "infinitesimal" in his work on motion. But how is this different from the very witty, "she [Zamira] unkierkegaarded little crooks from the province" (202/149) as a way of saying she removed from them their scruples?[14]

In *Una trappola di parole* [A Trap of Words], Carla Benedetti,[15] concerned with developing the tension between representation and representability, opposes the cognitive *groviglio* to Gadda's concept of non-being, the "undifferentiated darkness" which threatens the life of the individual, or, in the words of the *Pasticciaccio*, the abyss "where names thin out". A valuable aspect of her work is the awareness of self-critique in Gadda's style and the understanding of Gadda's enjoyment of his painful struggle with the "enigma of pain", with which she closes her study. She does not, however, connect story-telling and theorization, nor does she see in story-telling a possible bridge between male and female (123–142).

Marina Fratnik, in her complex and exhaustive study, *L'Écriture détournée: essay sur le texte narratif de C. E. Gadda*, offers extensive analysis of narrative organization in Gadda. She identifies the principle of his writing as "verbal derivation", the minimal alteration of semic structures which, in producing "tortuous trajectories", subverts the texts' own intended programs (XVII). This accounts for the Gaddian proliferation, which she sees as unsatisfied desire for the "right word". It would seem, therefore, that Fratnik's conceptual model for interpreting the pluralizing feature of Gadda's style is ultimately, though not obviously, related to a lack, a lack originating in the chasm between the sign and the signified. This lack, however, takes on a positive valence for Fratnik, and reality is honoured by the manifestation of language's incapacity to reach its referent (305). But if I am correct in this reading of Fratnik, then there seems to be some ontological difficulty inherent in her description of Gadda's technique, for total opacity of language would result in total linguistic inactivity.

Nevertheless, it may be possible to regard Fratnik's account as the realization within an entirely distinct interpretive system, a radically other discourse, of my own conclusions on knowledge and shame. To negotiate the differences on this point between Fratnik and myself would ultimately demand the full elaboration of an ontology of lack and excess, a subject central to the theories of Lacan, Derrida, and Deleuze and Guattari.

The *Pasticciaccio*'s form, Ragusa asserts, that of a detective novel, a detective novel without a solution, is particularly appropriate to Gadda's epistemological undertaking: "The 'mystery' is all about us. Gadda, being a scientist…, belonging to the race of post-metaphysical man, rejects the mystical and the supernatural. But the irrational, the subnatural or supernatural, takes its revenge and presents him with an epistemological problem. And so he creates Ingravallo, a detective whose business it is to ferret out knowledge and whose fate it is to remain ignorant" (142).

9

As for Gadda himself, he addresses, in his correspondence, a question that had become a critical locus: "[to say that] I did not finish the *Pasticciaccio* is the 'witticism' of some fine soul that maintains my incapacity to finish it" (Gadda Conti, 1974: 86). In an interview with Alberto Moravia, Gadda claims that "the refusal of the finished text" was due to his "conscious desire to close in dramatic apocope the story which tended to become deformed" (1976: 4–5). But in light of his theory of the constant deformation of reality and the deforming operation of knowing and representing reality, this can only be a joke, though delivered with a straight face. How else to interpret a remark from another interview, with Dacia Maraini? To her (Maraini, 19), he said, enigmatically, "the policeman understands who is the murderer and this suffices", and, more peculiarly, he added, "[t]he story was told me as true by a person I know, and who, I believe, wishes me no harm"! In both interviews, however, Gadda also offers more serious reasons. "The knot suddenly untangles itself, and it abruptly closes the story. I considered that dwelling on the 'how' and the 'why' would have been vain mumbling, pedantic dragging-on, and anyway posthumous to the end of the narrative" (1976: 5). And, more importantly, he addresses the issue of the reader's exhaustion: "I have interrupted the *Pasticciaccio* on purpose, because the *giallo*[16] must not be dragged on like certain artificial *gialli* which are prolonged ad nauseam and end by tiring the mind of the reader" (Maraini, ibid.). Here Gadda grounds his claim for the aesthetic unity of the *Pasticciaccio* in rejection of the 'normal' satisfactions of the detective genre. A novel about frustrated knowledge, *Quer pasticciaccio brutto de via Merulana* frustrates the epistemic expectations of its reader.

Conversely, from the perspective of the writer, his novel about frustrated desire (that of Liliàna Balducci, of the detective Ingravallo) involves also the frustration of narrative desire.[17] Narrative desire is blocked by the doubling-back of the plot. The exasperating doubles of the novel, which I shall later analyze, are a comment on frustration and fantasy in the erotics of writing. But this blocking, as it were, of the plot on the way to its end, germinates the intricate world of the *Pasticciaccio*, and the frustration of narrative desire forces its proliferation as style.

Ingravallo's *Praticaccia*

Erotics of the Declassed Male

The beginning of the novel establishes Ingravallo's status as an unusual detective, one of the youngest and yet one of the most envied of the homicide squad. He distinguishes himself, in the context of the story, from other policemen, from other men, from other people in general. In fact, Ingravallo's character may be said to be a major locus of difference. He has strong and unorthodox views about crime and criminals. He expresses them in rapid shots, "which crackled on his lips like the sudden illumination of a sulphur match" [che facevano sulla bocca il crepitio improvviso d'uno zolfanello illuminatore] (4/16), interrupting his habitual apparent sleepiness. They involve his particular kind of philosophy applied to crime:

> The opinion that we must 'reform within ourselves the meaning of the category of cause,' as handed down by the philosophers from Aristotle to Immanuel Kant, and replace cause with causes was for him a central, persistent opinion, almost a fixation.

> L'opinione che bisognasse 'riformare in noi il senso della categoria di causa' quale avevamo dai filosofi, da Aristotele o da Emmanuele Kant, e sostituire alla causa le cause era in lui una opinione centrale e persistente: una fissazione, quasi. (5/16)

Ingravallo believes in a multiplicity of causes overdetermining one crime:

> The apparent motive, the principal motive was, of course, single. But the ugly crime was the effect of a whole compass* of motives which had blown on it in a whirlwind (like the sixteen winds in the list of winds when they twist together in a tornado, in a cyclonic depression) and had ended by pressing into the vortex of the crime the enfeebled 'reason of the world.' Like wringing the neck of a chicken.

La causale apparente, la causale principe, era sì, una. Ma il fattaccio era l'effetto di tutta una rosa di causali che gli eran soffiate addosso a molinello (come i sedici venti della rosa dei venti quando s'avviluppano a tromba in una depressione ciclonica) e avevano finito per strizzare nel vortice del delitto la debilitata 'ragione del mondo.' Come si storce il collo a un pollo. (5-6/17)

This kind of *dictum* characterizes him, and it has real intellectual depth, but, of course, people think that he talks funny, that there is something not quite right in his approach to criminal cases. Such views, in the opinion of his police colleagues (both his superiors and his subordinates), come from reading strange books, from thinking crazy thoughts, and from using "words that mean nothing, or almost nothing, but which serve like no others* to dazzle the naive, the ignorant" [parole che non vogliono dir nulla, o quasi nulla, ma servono come non altre ad accileccare gli sprovveduti, gli ignari] (6/17).

Continuous with this is Ingravallo's linguistic fastidiousness. Thus, for example, his chief, Dottor Fumi, once too often corrected by Ingravallo for a mispronunciation ("'Cortina d'Ampiezzo...' 'D'Ampezzo', grumbled Ingravallo"), retorts: " 'D'Ampezzo, d'Ampezzo: all right, Ingravallo, you're our philosophy professor" [D'Ampezzo, d'Ampezzo: e vva buono, Ingravallo, vuie site nu professore 'e filosofia] (240/174). Even his landlady, a widow aspiring to a gentility of sorts, rejects in a practical manner his fussiness. Referring, towards the end of the novel, to Ingravallo's suffering for Liliana, she says, "such *anguirsh* for that poor soul, on your mind" [co quel pàtema della pover'anima in corpo], and, when as expected he corrects her, she reacts: "Anguish, anguirsh[18] … isn't it the same thing? You've had too much education, Doctor: you are like a school-teacher sometimes" [Pàtema, patéma… che? nun è la stessa cosa? Lei è tropp'istruito, sor dottó: me pare 'n maestro de scola] (366/261; italics mine)[19].

These differentiations set Ingravallo up as a 'displaced' character, but others show that his displacement has psycho-social significance: he is declassed. He does not think like one of his own class. His thought elevates and alienates him.

Already at the beginning of the novel, he is described as being poor, coming, as he does, from a poor Southern region (Molise),[20] and living on the meager salary of a government employee (3/15). Ironically, Ingravallo himself represents for his landlady her own desire to transcend her class level: for her he was that "most distinguished government employee", whom she has always dreamt of having as her tenant. As will become clear from the analysis of Ingravallo's relations with Liliana Balducci, it is unfortunate that only in his landlady's eyes does he have such status, for her wish alone cannot establish it, her regard for him must be qualified by her own – low – station in life.

When first introduced to Angeloni, a bureaucrat from the Ministry of National Economy, who will in time become his victim, Ingravallo's reaction to social status superior to his own is sarcastic, if not hostile:

The designated man bowed slightly: 'Commendatore Angeloni', he then ventured, on his own. 'Ingravallo,' Ingravallo said, who so far hadn't even been made a cavaliere, touching the brim of his hat with two fingers.

Il designato s'inchinò, leggermente: 'Commendator Angeloni,' proferì di se stesso. 'Ingravallo,' fece Ingravallo, che ancora non era neppure cavaliere, toccandosi con due diti l'ala del cappello. (40/40)

Later, when faced with the impudence of Giuliano Valdarena, Ingravallo experiences his distrust of Valdarena's story as social humiliation, as though Valdarena were mocking him "a flatfoot* that had not yet been made cavaliere" [questurino non ancora cavaliere] (159/119).

When his chief, Dottor Fumi, comes into the room on the morning of the Menegazzi theft, Ingravallo notices that he is wearing "a petal, a single white petal, in his button hole" [un petalo, un solo petalo bianco all'occhiello]. And he thinks, in dialect, "Almond blossom…, the first of the season. So now he can afford even* flowers" [Sciure 'e màndurlo…, (i)l primo della stagione. Mo ce pàveno pure ll'ammennole] (21/27).

This class humiliation becomes an erotics of abasement and aspiration when developed in sexual terms in the early dinner scene at the Balducci residence. When Ingravallo is struck by the two kinds of beauty offered by Liliana and her maid Assunta, it is his own status that comes out in the juxtaposition/opposition:

In that moment, both maid and mistress seemed extremely beautiful to Don Ciccio; the maid, harsher, had a severe, self-confident expression, a pair of steady, luminous eyes, two gems, a nose that made a straight line with the forehead: a Roman 'virgin' of the age of Clelia; and the mistress, such a cordial manner, such a lofty tone, so nobly passionate, so melancholy!…. Looking at her guest, those deep eyes … seemed to see, beyond the poor person of the 'officer,' all the poor dignity of a life! And she was *rich*, very *rich*, they said: her husband was well-off… . But she was even richer in her own right.

In quell'attimo sia la serva sia la padrona parvero a don Ciccio estremamente belle; la serva più aspra, aveva un'espressione severa, sicura, due occhi fermi, luminosissimi, quasi due gemme, un naso diritto con il piano della fronte: una 'vergine' romana dell'epoca di Clelia; la padrona un tratto così cordiale, un tono così alto, così nobilmente appassionato, così malinconico!… . Guardando l'ospite, quegli occhi fondi…, parevano scorgere, dietro la povera persona del 'dottore,' tutta la povera dignità di una vita! E lei era *ricca: ricchissima*, dicevano: suo marito stava bene… . Ma lei era ancora più ricca per conto suo. (9/19; emphases mine)

It is not by mere syntagmatic lexical progression, or mere association of ideas, that we go from Ingravallo's poor dignity of life to Liliana's material riches, nor is it a coincidence that he is attracted to both maid and mistress. It is through the tension mistress/maid[21] that

Ingravallo's declassment is revealed as erotic. He must repress "the admiration that Assunta aroused in him…, a fascination, an authority wholly Latin and Sabellian" [l'ammirazione che l'Assunta destava in lui…, un fascino, un imperio tutto latino e sabellico] (11/20), under the noble, melancholy gaze of the mistress, which

> seemed to dismiss mysteriously every improper phantom, establishing in one's soul* a harmonious discipline, like a music almost,* that is a texture of dreamed* architectures over the ambiguous derogations of the senses.

> pareva licenziare misteriosamente ogni fantasma improprio, istituendo per le anime una disciplina armoniosa: quasi una musica: cioè un contesto di sognate architetture sopra le derogazioni ambigue del senso. (11/20)

Interestingly, the "dreamed architectures" are nothing but the sublimation of the improper phantom: both the lust for the maid and the enchantment with Liliana are forms of the same psychic energy, of fantasy.

In fact, Liliana had once been, "with her kindness, her goodness, a charming…inspiration" [in bontà, in gentilezza: come una gentile…inspiratrice]. In the tradition of courtly love, Ingravallo had become a troubadour: he had once "ventured to write…a sonnet" [(aveva) tentato…un sonetto] (91/74). Liliana is, for Ingravallo, donna, Madonna-like, she is elevated.[22]

But her elevation is that of class,[23] and a pretty parvenu class at that: Liliana is not a member of some old blue-blooded aristocracy, but the daughter of a sharp-dealer, living in the "palace of gold, or of the sharks, if you prefer" [palazzo dell'Oro, o dei pescicani che fusse] (22/27).[24]

Ingravallo is defined against two types of 'real' males: the authoritative, older, father-like male, such as Liliana's husband, and the young stud (bully or dandy), towards whom he feels bitter jealousy and rancour.

It is with envious disdain that two of the male figures in Liliana's life, her husband, and her priest, are described with words related to each other both by root and by suffix: the husband is an "omaccio" (113/89), and her priest-confessor is an "omone". Both suffixes work to connote physical size and authority, qualities not possessed by Ingravallo. "One would have said that *in every big man* she venerated… an honorary father, a potential father, even in Don Lorenzo" [si sarebbe detto che in ogni omone lei venerasse… un padre onorario, un padre in potenza: anche in don Lorenzo] (13–14/22; italics mine), though neither is capable of inseminating Liliana, one as a result of "gamic", the other of sacramental, incompatibility.

As for the second type,

> there was, painful as it is to admit, in Don Ciccio a certain coldness, a kind of prickly jealousy towards the young, especially towards handsome young men, and even more so, the sons of the rich.

14

[c]'era, duole dirlo, in don Ciccio, una certa freddezza, come un'astiosa gelosia verso i giovani, specie i bei giovani, e tanto più i figli dei ricchi. (17–8/25)

He is not 'handsome' and cannot even "console himself with that proverb he had heard in Milan from a girl at the clinic for venereal diseases in Via delle Oche: 'Real men are always good-lookers.' " [consolarsi con quel proverbio che aveva udito a Milano da una ragazza, al dispensario celtico di via delle Oche: 'I òmen hin semper bèi'] (18/25).[25]

Nor can he escape the painful blow dealt him when his native province was excluded from the map of Italian male potency made by a famous sexologist:

He remembered that one of the two great erotologists, but he didn't recall which one, had become transformed into a geodesist, and had considered the wisdom of drawing up a map of the male contour line ....This territory ... of the highest level of male potency was... a spheric triangle, or rather, a geodetic one. And the vertices, the extreme geodetic strongholds of the unmatchable triangle, he, Norman Douglas, or he, Lawrence, saw as emerging from the three cities of Reggio (Calabria), Sassari, and Civitavecchia... .'He could have moved a little farther north, this dick... ologist,'* Ingravallo thought silently, clenching his teeth in anger: 'and a little more to the east,' his unconscious prompted him, 'to the top of the Matese mountains.'[26]

Gli sovvenne che uno dei due grandi erotologi, ma non realizzava quale, un bel giorno, s'era tramutato in geodeta, e aveva considerato l'opportunità di redigere una mappa delle isoipse maschili... .Codesto territorio ...di più eccelso livello del potenziale maschile, era... un triangolo sferico, o meglio geodetico. E i vertici, i capisaldi geodetici estremi dell'ineguagliabile triangolo, lui, Norman Douglas, o lui, Lawrence, li riconosceva emergere dalle tre città di Reggio (Calabria), Sassari e Civitavecchia... .'Poteva arrivé nu poco chiù a Norte, sto minch... iòlogo,' ideò muto Ingravallo strizzando i denti dalla rabbia: 'spingersi nu poco chiù a levante,' gli suggerì l'inconscio, 'fino in coppa a 'o Matese.' (24/175)

Of Giuliano, Liliana's cousin, Ingravallo has the horrible suspicion that he might have been her lover, and worse, might even have been paid for his services. He is a good looking boy, "lucky with women", who "haunted* him in swarms, buzzing around him; they fell on him, all together, nose-diving, like so many flies on a honeycomb" [lo perseguitavano a sciami, a volo radente: e gli precipitavano poi addosso tutte insieme, e in picchiata, come tante mosche sul miele] (78/66). Among them, the cousin would count Liliana. If her religion had allowed it, he says, " 'well, I'm sure that she would have fallen in love with me, that she would have loved me madly... . Like all the others.' " ['be', son certo che si sarebbe innamorata di me, che mi avrebbe amato pazzamente... . Come tutte'] (147/111).

Likewise, Diomede Lanciani, Ines' boyfriend and pimp, is followed by his 'beauties,' who, says Ines, "would go to the end of the earth to hunt for him" [L'annerebbero a cercà puro in capo ar monno]. Ingravallo does not fail to make the connection: " 'He too! He, too!' Ingravallo's feelings ached. 'In the roster of the fortunate and the happy, even he!' His face became grim. 'He, too, pursued* by women!' " ['Anche lui, anche lui!' dolorò Ingravallo in suo sentire. 'Nel novero de' fortunati e felici, anche lui!' Il volto gli si fece tetro. 'Anche lui! Perseguito dalle donne!'] (227/165).[27]

A double equation evolves and is reinforced throughout, from which Ingravallo is excluded: class is money, and money is sex. This connection is made explicit in the disquisitions of Liliana's aunts, after her death, in their acerbic accusation of husband Balducci: notwithstanding his reputation of virile 'hunter', he has squandered, not only Liliana's beauty, but also her wealth. For them, his misuse of "his bride's carnal and dotal* validity" [validità carnale e dotale de su moje] is twofold, because

the gamic[28] unit... also includes as well an economic quantum.* She was a splendid girl, and there was a coffer of jewels: former and latter ripened by the years: by the slow, tacit years. She was a girl with a little box; and they, the Valdarenas, had entrusted the husband with the key: and the right to make use of it, clickety-click: the sacrosanct usufruct.*

l'unità gamica... include altresì un quanto economico. Era una splendida figliola, ed era un cofano di gioie: l'una e l'altro maturati dagli anni: dai lenti, taciti anni. Era una figliola, con una scatoluccia: di cui loro, i Valdarena, avevano affidato ar marito la chiavicina: e il diritto di servirsene, tric, tric: il santo usufrutto. (115/90)

The economic quantum thus is identified with Ingravallo's ubiquitous 'quantum of eros' (6/17).

The equation is painfully felt by Ingravallo. From the abundance of her gentleness (beauty/wealth), Liliana is perhaps the only woman to have ever shown him 'generosity', that generosity of which the pompous, rather vulgar husband boasts post-prandially: "Women, of course, when they're in love.... don't bother about petty details; they're generous-minded then . . .. They give, they give freely* " [Le donne, se sa, quanno so' innamorate... non badano a certe miserie. Hanno le vedute larghe.... Largheggiano, largheggiano] (91/74).

The iteration, indicating a sort of blown-up male self-complacency, will be echoed by a further piece of investigation. In it, what is important is Ingravallo's reaction to the theories of a nameless executive of the oil company for which Giuliano works, who contends that clients must be treated like women – seduced and forced into fidelity – and then, going on to the next logical metaphor, says: "And all screwing aside, those who love us, follow us.... . So, I mean, they pay. They pay up" [E poi, corna a parte, chi ci ama ci segue... . Allora, voglio dire, pagano. Pagano senza rifiatare]. "They pay. They pay" [Pagheno, pagheno] (108/85), thinks Ingravallo.

Unlike Giuliano, who since he "isn't hard up for money, can't be very hard up for the other thing" [si nun è a corto di quatrini, d'antro nun po' esse tanto a corto], Ingravallo had "come from years of poverty, of hardship, from the barren Matese mountain... a humble[29] and dogged investigator of events, or of souls, in the law's name" [venuto da poveri, duri anni, dallo scarno monte Matese... misero e pertinace indagatore dei fatti, o delle anime, secondo la legge]. (78/65–6)

All those other men operate on one class level, their own, while Ingravallo is alienated, declassed. The reason for his frustration lies in the desire to transcend his own class, the desire to get a woman of a different class.

Ingravallo's sexual frustration is hence not merely the impotent potency of a man not getting any, but a gender dislocation. Declassing short-circuits the simple polarity male/female. The sublimation called forth by the beauty of Liliana complicates eros. The polarity is broken up by displacement and reversal. Ingravallo is no longer simply a male polarized against females. Another term is introduced, both in relation to Assunta and to Liliana. With regard to Assunta, the maid, Ingravallo (who, as policeman, should in fact be a "frequenter of maids" [68/58]), is seen having to repress desire, shifting, under Liliana's gaze, his erotic energy from the maid to her mistress, sublimating it.[30] Furthermore, Liliana – whose name symbolizes purity, and to whom, in fact, Virginia once says: "Oh, my beautiful* signora Liliana, you are [like] a Madonna for me!" [Sora mia bella Liliana, voi site 'a madonna pe mme!] (185/137) – is, to all intents and purposes, a virgin.[31]

The class/sex tangle presents itself in a near music. Ingravallo posits psychic harmony in an imagined order. One fantasy has bought out the other.[32]

That women are not part of his life is first announced, even if under the guise of a joke, a play on language, in the manner in which the daily *Messaggero* had phrased his landlady's ad for the room he will rent: at the end of the advertised text we read: "women excluded*" [escluse donne] (4/15). Gadda draws our attention to the sylleptic usage of this pronouncement by commenting that this injunction "in the language of the *Messaggero*'s advertisements can offer, as everyone knows, a double interpretation" [nel gergo delle inserzioni del *Messaggero* offre, com'è noto, una duplice possibilità d'interpretazione] (4/15). The double interpretation does not really refer to either 'no women need apply,' or 'no women permitted after dark' or something of the sort. Rather, it organizes proleptically a symbolic paradox, whose fulfillment will be actualized only when the novel is finished and we look back at Ingravallo's relation to its women. There is a double meaning – of knowing and yet not having women – which will continue to contaminate the rest of the text. This description of the detective's credentials immediately precedes the affirmation that

a certain familiarity with the ways of the world, with our so-called 'Latin' world...must have been his: a certain knowledge of men: and of women.

una certa praticaccia del mondo, del nostro mondo detto 'latino'... doveva di certo avercela: una certa conoscenza degli uomini: e delle donne. (3/15)

Enforcing this double meaning, we find the case of Maresciallo Santarella, "one of the two centaurs" (210) of the Alban rural branch of the national police force, the Royal Carabinieri. He is a rival, as it were, of Ingravallo, who belonged to the other branch, the urban police (the Questura). Santarella's story, counters and so emphasizes the significance of "no women allowed", validating the paradox of Ingravallo. A most virile specimen, Santarella lives with no fewer than nine women:

> his wife, her old blind mother and her slightly feeble-minded sister, a sister of his own, unmarried and totaly chaste*...: three daughters, not yet of an age not to be chaste, and two tenants, twin sisters, *quondam* on the verge of unchastity,* but by now [after the congruent skipping town of the hoped-for dechastizer...], now definitely returned to chastity.

> la moglie, la di lei vecchia madre cieca e la di lei sorella un po' scema, una sorella propria, illibatissima...: tre figlie, non ancora in età da non essere illibate, e due subinquiline, due gemelle, quondam in procinto di disillibarsi, ma oggimai [dopo congruo taglio di corda dello sperato disillibatore...], oggimai definitivamente rientrate nella illibazione. (211/155)

In his house, "of the male element...there was only himself" [(d)i maschio, in casa sua, non c'era che lui]. In fact, when he decides to rent "because of the times and the opportunity and his pay, a small portion of his penetralia" [in ragion de' tempi e dell'opportunità e della paga, una esuberata porzioncina de' penetrali], he puts an ad in the same daily, *Il Messaggero*. He does not have, however,

> the heart to assert to the readers 'no women,' that cruel 'halt!' of the landlady of Ingravallo. No, no, no, in his house... quite the contrary: women there were: and women there would be.[33]

> l'animo di poter intimare a' leggitori l' 'escluse donne!,' quel crudel 'alto là!' della padrona di casa d'Ingravallo. No, no, no, in casa sua... tutt'al contrario: donne erano: e donne sarebbero. (211/155)

In short, Ingravallo is unlucky with women, and his personal sexual frustration must bear upon the theme of the failed relation which is at work throughout the story.

"No women" in the body of the text not only comes right after the reference to Ingravallo's knowledge of men and women, it also comes right before a reiteration of this knowledge and thus is reinforced by its positioning. The second time there is an added element: Ingravallo is said to "enunciate some theoretical idea (a general idea, of course*) on the affairs of men: and of women" [enunciare qualche teoretica idea (idea generale s'intende) sui casi degli uomini: e delle donne] (4/16; emphases mine). The interdiction "no women" is made once again. For he knows about women, but what kind of knowing is this, with no women in it? if it is only a purely theoretical knowledge, related to the absence of women? Derailed in his desire for Assunta, frustrated in his desire for Liliana, by his declassment and his dislocation, Ingravallo is forced into theorizing.

The Erotics of Theory as Male

As Alba Andreini points out, Ingravallo's "refusal of facile certainties" and "autonomous thinking activity" (122) differentiate Ingravallo from his colleagues. He is forever plagued by suspicion and skepticism, and his doubts, moreover, are not the kind just anybody might have, but his own, most "Ingravallian" doubts (19/26), part of a continuum of a specific mode of thought.

Known for his sudden theoretic pronouncements on crime, Ingravallo holds a highly abstract thesis about causation as knot:

> He sustained, among other things, that unforeseen catastrophes are never the consequence or the effect, if you prefer, of a single motive, of a cause singular; but they are rather like a whirlpool, a cyclonic point of depression in the consciousness of the world, towards which a whole multitude of converging causes have contributed. He also used words like knot or tangle, or muddle, or gnommero, which in Roman dialect means skein.

> Sosteneva fra l'altro, che le inopinati catastrofi non sono mai la conseguenza o l'effetto che dir si voglia d'un unico motivo, d'una causa al singolare: ma sono come un vortice, un punto di depressione ciclonica nella coscienza del mondo, verso cui hanno cospirato tutta una molteplicità di causali convergenti. Diceva anche nodo, o groviglio, o garbuglio, o gnommero, che alla romana vuol dire gomitolo. (5/16; emphases in the English translation)

Ingravallo believes that we must " 'reform within ourselves the meaning of the category of cause,' as handed down by the philosophers from Aristotle to Immanuel Kant, and replace cause with causes" ['riformare in noi il senso della categoria di causa' quale avevamo dai filosofi, da Aristotele o da Emmanuele Kant, e sostituire alla causa le cause] (5/16). But the concept of the knot itself is found in Aristotle, and is related to that of *aporia*, difficulty of enquiry (literally, "doubt") (*Metaphysics*, Book 3, 995a: 27–33): "there is no solution when the knot" which binds the intelligence "remains unknown". Moreover, "the difficulty of the mind shows precisely this, the existence of the knot in the matter at hand", in the object of enquiry.[34] The significance of this theory for our text lies, I think, in Gadda's unavowed – but likely – acquaintance with it, and his 'secret' use of it in terms of the novel's solution, as well as of the more important insolubility of the 'woman question.'

Ingravallo's police colleagues, in their "justified" criticisms of him, contend that notions like his and "philosophizing are to be left to scribblers" [le filosoficherie son da lasciare ai trattatisti].[35] What they oppose to his theories are the more pragmatic "sense of responsibility, prompt decision, civil moderation" [senso di responsabilità e decisione sicura, moderazione civile], patience, and yes, "a strong stomach" [uno stomaco pur anche a posto]. What they oppose to Ingravallo's abstract theorizing is practice: "the practical experience of the police stations and the homicide squad" [la pratica dei commissariati e della squadra mobile], which is "quite another thing" [tutt'un altro affare] (4/17).

Yet, police practice includes also crimes designated Ingravallo's (" 'his crimes' " [i 'suoi' delitti]), special in that they are knots: "When they call *me*... Sure. If they call me, you can be sure that there's trouble: some mess, some *gliuommero*[36] to untangle" [Quanno me chiammeno!... Già. Si me chiammeno a me... può stà ssicure ch'è nu guaio: quacche gliuommero... de sberretà] (5/16; italics in the English translation).

And his knots, conversely, are special in that they are crimes, the kind of complex and ugly messes (the *pasticciaccio brutto* of the title) for which he has developed not only a theory but also a knowing practice, a practical knowledge. Ingravallo possesses not the mere pratica, but a *praticaccia*,[37] a knowing practice: "a certain familiarity with the ways of the world, with our so-called 'Latin' world" [una certa praticaccia del mondo, del nostro mondo detto 'latino'] (3/15).

To the ugly mess (*pasticciaccio*), corresponds an ugly knowledge. It is not an accident that the same linguistic suffix augmentation is used for both: the word play, a specialty of Gadda's, calls attention to their apposition.

Further, in Detective Ingravallo's theory and practice, women have a definite function: " 'you're sure to find skirts where you don't want to find them'. A belated Italian revision of the trite 'cherchez la femme' " ['ch'i femmene se retroveno addó n'i vuò truvà.' Una tarda riedizione italica del vieto 'cherchez la femme']. In every crime, in every *pasticciaccio*, there is "a quantum of 'eros' " [un quanto di erotia] (6/17). Ingravallo's *praticaccia* is of men, *and of women*:

A certain familiarity with the ways of the world, with our so-called 'Latin' world...must have been his: a certain knowledge of men: *and of women*.

Una certa praticaccia del mondo, del nostro mondo detto 'latino'... doveva di certo avercela: una certa conoscenza degli uomini: *e delle donne*. (3/15; italics mine)

The detective's abstractions are a mode of sensibility, of knowing the world, the ugly, messy world of crime. The *praticaccia* is, as the last quotation shows, a *conoscenza*, a knowledge the privileged object of which is woman.[38]

Women are always part of the mess. Cherchez la femme. The quest for knowledge is the search for a woman, for woman. Women represent the object of Ingravallo's quest for knowledge, a quest that like the desire determining it, must remain unfulfilled, since to make an object object of knowledge is to create a mystery. Woman is made the trope of mystery.

At the center of the mess on via Merulana, there is Liliana Balducci. By her death, the tangle to be unraveled is revealed; but in this most untraditional *giallo*, the process of untangling will not, ultimately, reveal her. Even before her death, she presents to Ingravallo a veiled, secret sorrow, an enigma. She is described as concealed, desirable but unattainable in her distance, enveloped in an aura of noble melancholy. As she walks in the erotic atmosphere of the streets of Rome, at dusk, she is "[a] woman who seemed veiled... lost, at times, in some private dream" [(d)onna quasi velata... assorta, a volte, in un suo sogno] (20/26).

She does not confide in Ingravallo (in fact, throughout the novel, she barely speaks at all). He is irresistibly drawn to interpret. From slight yet telling clues, he intuits, he puts together a case, he forms a theory. He reads, as it were, the signs of a contingent mystery, and in relation to it will construct his own story as well.

He believes he has penetrated, as it were, the mystery her own husband, "the old goat, Balducci, the husband* " [il caprone, Balducci uomo] (7/18), had not:

> One would have said, if one felt like fantasticating, that Balducci had not val-
> ued,* had not penetrated all her beauty: all that was noble and *recondite* in
> her: and so* ... the children had not come.

> Si sarebbe detto, a voler fantasticare, ch'egli, il Balducci non avesse valutato,
> non avesse penetrato tutta la bellezza di lei: quanto vi era in lei di *recondito* e
> allora... i figli non erano arrivati. (13/21; italics mine)

At the center of this mess is Liliana Balducci's unfulfilled maternity, exacerbated by the ideological context of "son-loving Fascism".[39] This interpretation will be confirmed to Ingravallo by the testimony he gathers after her death.

But this secret's revelation is no revelation at all, since the mystery that Ingravallo will never penetrate is the mystery of her subjectivity, of her being as desiring subject, the living subjectivity that will be necessarily negated as it is transformed by Ingravallo's desiring quest into an object of knowledge. His *conoscenza* is mystification as well as knowledge.

With her death, Ingravallo's attempt to master her elusive subjectivity will be rendered both formally possible and irremediably impossible. Discovered murdered, she is no longer subject, she becomes a thing, a "horrible thing" [cosa orribile] (67/58), her body has "the immobility of an *object*... of a disfigured dummy" [immutabilità di un *oggetto*... d'uno sfigurato manichino] (68/59; italics mine). In a posture of utter exposure, her body is offered up to him, in a sort of "horrible invitation" [invito orribile] (69/59). In death, her objectification achieves its limiting case.

During the course of his investigations, Ingravallo's gaze remains unchallenged. The confusion the police photographers create around her body appears to the detective

the first hum of eternity over her opaque senses, that body of a woman which no longer possessed modesty or memory… . The beauty, the clothing, the spent flesh of Liliana were there: the sweet body, still clothed from their gaze.

il primo ronzare dell'eternità sui sensi opachi di lei, de quer corpo de donna che nun ciaveva più pudore né memoria… . La bellezza, l'indumento, la spenta carne di Liliana era là: il dolce corpo, rivestito ancora agli sguardi. (84/69)

Not challenging the gaze, but forever closed in death, in "the chill of the sarcophagus and of the taciturn final abode" [gelo del sarcofago e delle taciturne dimore] (68/58),[40] Liliana refuses herself, she resists. She may be possessed as object of knowledge, but her corpse is the limit of that knowledge.

Ingravallo sees the violence done to Liliana, the cut throat, the blood, the open, sunken eyes looking nowhere, the skirt thrown back. His gaze uncovers her, in a repetition of the movements of her killer. He imagines the moment of her death, when she "had yielded* herself to the slaughterer" [si era concessa al carnefice]. He imagines "her throat,… completely bare and undefended*" [la gola… interamente nuda e indifesa] (82/68), her scratched face, "resigned to the will of Death" [rassegnata alla volontà della Morte] (70/60).

Most powerfully, he imagines the murderer's gaze, and how it must have frightened her: "the eyes! of the endless beast. The unsuspected ferocity of the world…was revealed to her all of a sudden…" [gli occhi! della belva infinita. La insospettata ferocia delle cose… le si rivelava d'un subito…] (82/68). Unimpeded, he gazes upon her body, and in his mind, he sees, sees even (he imagines) into her seeing, sees into the fierce gaze of the murderer that becomes one with his own. He lays claim to her living fear, astonishment, sight, as it becomes that dead thing, the thought of the other. Thus, all the while, in parallel psychic moves, the detective himself victimizes Liliana Balducci.

Just so does Liliana become his object when he undertakes a series of interrogations, "a kind of tormented salvage operation…" [una specie di tormentoso recupero…] (169/126), in which the men in Liliana's life (the husband, the cousin, the priest) act as her interpreters, giving her the voice she never had, a voice that is not hers.[41]

In his obsessive unveiling, Ingravallo also invents her, veiling Liliana again. He looks, he imagines, he reconstructs, he theorizes: "the female personality" [la personalità femminile], he mumbles to himself, "what did it all mean?…the female personality, typically gravity-centered on the ovaries" [che vvulive dì? 'a personalità femminile, tipicamente centrogravitata sugli ovarii]. And he easily, too easily, gives the answer: "the eminently echolalic quality of her soul" [la qualità eminamente ecolalica della di lei anima…] – because, as we know, she was conceded a soul, adds Gadda, by the Council of Mainz in 589 A.D. –

induces her to flutter gently around the axis of marriage: impressionable wax, she asks the seal of his imprint: from* the husband, the word and the affect, the ethos and the pathos.*

la induce a soavemente farfallare d'attorno al perno del coniugio: plastile cera, chiede dal sigillo l'impronta: al marito il verbo e l'affetto, l'ethos e il pathos. (139/106)

When the husband tries to explain her, he does no more than parody Ingravallo's own theorizing: he expounds freely about

the delicacy of the feminine soul and, in general, [about] woman's great sensitivity: which among those poor creatures is something diffused!* The word 'diffused' he had read in Milan, in the *Secolo*, in an article by Maroccus... the *Secolo*'s doctor: superlative!*

la delicatezza dell'animo femminile e, in genere, su quella gran sensitività della donna: che in loro, povere creature! è una cosa diffusa. Il 'diffusa' l'aveva letto a Milano, sur *Secolo*, in un articolo di Maroccus... er dottore der *Secolo*: finissimo! (69/126)

Contemptuous of the husband's vulgarity, Ingravallo will yet adopt Balducci's theory, adding, however, a most significant bit of his own:

all of them women, with *diffuse* sensitivity*.... Women all, both in their memories and their hope, and in the hard, obstinate pallor of their reticence and the purple of their non-confiteor.

femmine tutte, a *sensibbilità diffusa*.... Femmine tutte, e nel ricordo e nella speranza, e nel pallore duro e ostinato della reticenza e nella porpora del non-confiteor. (170/127; italics in the original)

It is this reticence, her unyielding refusal to "confess", with which Ingravallo was faced while Liliana was alive, which the silence of her death continually repeats.

At the end of the book, he again will look for an impossible knowledge, reproducing on a smaller scale what he has done to Liliana. He interrogates Assunta, Liliana's beautiful maid. Already sensing his defeat, he tries maniacally to interpret her role in the crime: "He tried, he tried to sum up, rationally; to pull the threads, one might say, of the inert puppet of the Probable" [Cercava, cervcava, di tirar le somme a ragione: di tirare i fili, si sarebbe detto, dell'inerte burattino del probabile] (382/272; italics mine). He madly accuses Assunta of knowing the name of the murderer or even of having killed Liliana herself, but she too resists:

'No, sir, no, Doctor: it wasn't me!' the girl implored then, simulating, perhaps, and in part enjoying,[42] a dutiful fear: the fear that whitens the face a little, but still resists all threats.

'No, sor dottò, no, no, nun so' stata io!' implorò allora la ragazza, simulando forse, e in parte godendo, una paura di dovere: quella che nu poco sbianca il visetto, e tuttavia resiste a minacce. (388/276)

The name of the maid means "the assumpted", referring to a quality of the Virgin Mary. The end of the novel, with its resistance of the Virgin-like Assunta, comes full circle, executes the closure of the "women excluded" theme, Ingravallo's never-ending torment. And so, he can no longer know. He is stopped in his tracks, and repents: "the incredible cry blocked the haunted man's fury" [il grido incredibile bloccò il furore dell'ossesso]:

That black, vertical fold above the two eyebrows of rage, in the pale white face of the girl, paralyzed him,[43] prompted him to reflect: to repent, almost.

Quella piega nera verticale tra i due sopraccigli dell'ira, nel volto bianchissimo della ragazza, lo paralizzò, lo indusse a riflettere: a ripentirsi, quasi. (388/276)

Is Ingravallo's penitence for Assunta, or is it for Liliana? Does he finally see himself, in his desire for her, in his attempt to penetrate her mystery, as the violator? Does he repent the crime of her death, which he has repeated in making her subjectivity the object of his knowledge? This seems to be the case, because what Ingravallo repents is his *theory* of Liliana, of women, in general. Already in the first exposition of his Italic version of 'cherchez la femme,' we read:

And then he seemed to repent, as if he had slandered the females,* and wanted to change his mind. But that would have got him into difficulties. So he would remain silent and pensive, as if afraid of having said too much.

e poi pareva pentirsi, come d'aver calunniato 'e femmene, e voleva mutare idea. Ma allora si sarebbe andati nel difficile. Sicché taceva pensieroso, come temendo d'aver detto troppo. (6/17)

And it is this almost repentance, this seeming repentance, that Gadda refuses, fails, to represent. Undecidable, it passes into silence, with the ending of the novel.

III Gadda and the Hyposapphic Hymn

Ingravallo's veiling/violation of Liliana is paralleled by the police interrogation of the prostitute Ines Cionini. Thought to be the link between the city and the countryside from which Liliana's so-called nieces, and probably her killer, came, Ines is brought into the cold, enormous room at police headquarters where most of the agents involved in the investigation are present.

From the very beginning, she is, in all her dereliction, an object of desire. She brings with her "a gust of the wild" [una ventata di selvatico] (197/145). Her body, though incredibly dirty and dressed in rags, amplifies "for all those underfed males*" [a tutti quei maschi di poca cena],

> 'in the minds of the on-lookers,'* that is, for the male delirium..., the stupen-
> dous suggestion:... the true and basic sense of the life of the viscera, of
> hunger: and of animal warmth.

> al 'pensiero degli astanti,' cioè al maschile delirare quel suggerimento
> stupendo:... il senso vero e fondo della vita dei visceri, della fame: e del calore
> animale. (199/147)

What they think she offers, with her child's eyes, is "the name of a happiness that was yet possible; a joy, a hope, a truth superior to their papers" [il nome d'una felicità tuttavia possibile; d'una gioia, d'una speranza, d'una verità superordinata alle cartoffie] (199/147).

Desire and desire to know, once again, merge, and once again, a story will be forced out:

> Love, after besmirching her, had handed her over to the which of hunger. All,
> now, hoped to find in her the longed-for peep-hole* of whom they had need.
> She understood this; she knew it: and for the matter, hell, who gives a damn?
> the evil that the sky-blue days* had poured over her was such that she had to
> give it back, to her protectors. So, she sang.

L'amore, dopo averla insudiciata, l'aveva regalata alla ventura della fame. Tutti, ora, speravano di trovare in lei la desideratissima spia di cui avevano bisogno. Lei lo capiva, lo sapeva: del resto, bah, chi se ne frega? il male che i giorni azzuri le avevano rovesciato addosso era tanto, che bisognava ricambiarglielo, ai protettori. Cicalò, sicché. (200/147)

Ines tells the police what they want to know, she presents herself to them as known, and thus she resists, in a time-honoured manner of woman, being invaded: " 'With these cops, a girl never knows.' Maybe it was better to satisfy them, she thought… . That would be the end of it, at least!" ['Con questi nun se sa mai.' Forse era meglio contentarli, pensò… . Sarebbe finita, armeno!] (234/170). She plays their game. One by one, the movements of the interrogators, of persuasion, supplication, threat, humiliation, are matched by her evasions, lies, denials, and admissions.

What seems to break her down, however, is their gaze,[44] in which their desire and desire to know converge:

But the men, those men, blackmailed her with their gaze alone, afire, broken at intervals by signals and flashes, not pertinent to the case, of a repugnant greed. Those men, from her, wanted to hear, to know.

Ma gli uomini, quegli uomini, la ricattavano col solo sguardo, acceso e rotto a intervalli, dai segni e dai lampi, non pertinenti alla pratica, di una cupidità ripugnante. Quegli uomini, da lei, volevano udire, sapere. (233–34/170)

She tries to hide her abject pain and shame behind "the rips, the tears, the wretched bunting, the sordid poverty of her dress" [le sdruciture, gli strappi, la misera stamigna, la sordida povertà del vestito] (233/169). She, who at first appeared to them as "a rather well-supplied girl" [una ragazza piuttosto provveduta del suo] (197/145), comes to feel

as if she were naked, *destitute*,*[45] before those who have the power to pry into the nakedness of shame and, if they don't mock it, they pass judgment on it: naked, destitute: as are all sons and daughters without shelter and without support, in the bestial arena of the earth.

nuda, *sprovveduta*, avanti a chi ha facoltà d'inquisire la nudità della vergogna e, se pur non la irride, la giudica: nuda, sprovveduta, come sono i figli e le figlie senza ricovero e senza sovvento, nell'arena bestiale della terra. (232-33/169; italics mine)

Exposed, violated, yet ever evasive, at the end of the interrogation, Ines recovers her composure, looks back at her "inquisitors" (167), stands erect and speaks "with a calm, ringing voice" [con voce calma, sonora] (254/184).

In this powerfully written scene, once more, a woman's subjectivity is at stake. Once more, the occasion of male power in the text resolves itself into power to desire, to uncover and thus to construct. Like Liliana, she has been made into an object of knowledge, and like Liliana she has somehow worked her own *non-confiteor*.

The parallelism with Liliana is, however, incomplete. My analysis of the two stories, up to this point, stops at epistemic violation and veiling. But what is there in Ines' story that would correspond to Liliana's death, to her total closure, which cannot be violated?

In order to answer this, we must look at Gadda himself, at the ultimate power, which is the power of the author, for whom all the events of the plot, of the text, constitute the pretexts of power.

It is my belief that, unlike authors who unquestioningly lay claim to fear and the representation of fear, and hence to the sovereign nature of their power,[46] Gadda experiences his own power to portray pain and shame as being sadistic,[47] morally questionable, that Gadda's giving us access to Ines' suffering is accompanied by his suffering at doing so, that not her objectification, but his own shame is at work as part of her portrayal.[48] Encoded in the text is a higher level of consciousness. And though the shame at the act of writing works throughout the novel, it is the interrogation of Ines that specifically articulates the author's preoccupation with the power of knowledge, completing the parallelism with the story of Liliana and Ingravallo. The story of Ines is a hyper-parallelism, a meta-level enactment of the power of representation and its consequences.

An analysis of two subtexts integrated to the interrogation of Ines will locate Gadda's relation to his own writing. In a digressive section, interrupting the story of Ines (but not its metonymical progress), Maresciallo Santarella is described roaming the countryside on his motor-bike in pursuit of his more or less official goals. As he rides, he contemplates the white caravans of clouds, also rushing, though no *reale* (policeman) is pursuing them. Still, they are "hooked" by the tips of the roof antennae, which "rip" them, tear them in a "perpetual deformability" [perpetua deformabilità].[49] Given their diaphanous nature, the clouds are highly penetrable, yet fleeting, "the fleeting, snowy flock" [il fuggente, niveo gregge], protecting behind them "cold shreds of blue-sky" [freddi brani di azzuro]. It is the shreds, these ruptured "fragments", that cannot be ultimately reconstructed into discrete, knowable, units: they constantly regroup, they recompose themselves: "then [they] closed themselves up again" [poi si richiudevano], and, moreover, "closed themselves up again in an *unreachable alternation of presages*, with the high wind..." [si richiudevano in una *irragiungibile alternazione di presagi*, col vento alto...] (218/159; italics mine). [50]

That this description's role is proleptic,[51] that it *anticipates* something, is suggested by the very use of the word *presagi*.[52] What it anticipates is the consummation of its metaphoric force in the second questioning of Ines. Ines has been pursued by the relentless police interrogators, unlike the clouds which are not followed by any policeman. But exactly like the scraps of sky, reclosing themselves behind the shreds of clouds, Ines will draw herself together once again.[53]

A second passage, part of the second round of questioning, reinforces, through semantic variations and repetition of certain key words, this reading: Ines, disregarding the gaze of the supreme authority (*Er Zignore*), is described, somewhat in explanation of her present circumstance, as having taken the path of love and consequently, of self-destruction:

When he [God] had called her by name, the name of her baptism, three times: Ines! Ines! Ines! at the beginning of her life in the underbrush, three times! like the Persons of the Holy Trinity... the oaks writhed in foreboding under the gusts of the masterful wind...[54]

Quando (Dio) l'aveva chiamata per nome, il nome del battesimo, tre volte, Ines! Ines! Ines! al principiare della macchia, tre volte! quante so' le Perzone de la Trinità... le querci si storcevano in presagi sotto le raffiche del vento maestro... (233/169)

The *querci*, bent, distorted but not broken, stand for the clouds and the sky that perdure behind the deforming power of the *vento maestro*. Ripping apart here becomes mere bending, distortion, resistance. So Ines, torn as she may seem, under the masterful blows of male investigation, will recompose her self, will stand erect again and close herself in the *irragiungibile alternazione* (unreachable alternation) of her subjectivity.

The question that I continue to ask myself is, what level of awareness is operative in Gadda's representation of female subjectivity?

If we go back to the account of Santarella's trip into the Alban countryside, we come upon a set of significant terms introduced by Gadda. Santarella is described as an enthusiastic life member of the newly founded motor Touring Club of Italy, the refrain of whose theme song he sings as he rides: "Ahead, Ahead, Away!" [Avanti, avanti, via!] (217/159; translation mine).

This song, says Gadda, had been born to the "hypocarduccian-hyposapphic muse" [alla musa ipocarducciano-iposàffica] of Signor Giovanni Bertacchi, poet laureate, as it were, of the Touring Club. The first level of meaning of these epithets is lack of literary value. The song is *hypo*, beneath, that is to say inferior in literary power to the works of Sappho, and even to those of Carducci, a turn of the century poet who employed classical verse forms, among which the sapphic meter. Moreover, Santarella brings to the septenary "una *ipo*tetica mèlode", a *hypo*thetical melos (217/139), not really a melody at all, no real music. Thus the whole hymn signifies *hypo*, pronounced inferiority. But Gadda's text emphasizes not merely the *hypo*, but also the "sapphic". Sappho, not Carducci, her 'imitator,' appears here as a model of literary excellence, and the force of her presence in this text can further be read as emblem of female subjectivity through a specific intertextual linkage of the interrogation of Ines with the framing images I have discussed.

A famous fragment of Sappho's monodies, found in the *Orations* of Maximus of Tyre (18.9), reads:

Eros shakes my wits, as the mountain wind attacks the oaks. [55]

28

Here we have the oaks bending in the wind, the very oaks we find in Ines' initiation in the underbrush.

While I have developed the sense in which the oaks will stand again (just as the fragmented sky will recompose), imaging the integrity of female subjectivity, Sappho's poem would seem to suggest rather the opposite, the dispersal of subjectivity, the dispersal of the integrity of subjectivity by Eros, the wind that shakes the oaks. But, behind its evocation of dispersal, it is Sappho's poem itself that perdures as expression of desiring subjectivity.

Thus the theme of female subjectivity as power of desire is reiterated, and it is impossible to doubt that this association is operative in Gadda's text. This fragment is one of the best known from Sappho, and Gadda's knowledge of the classics is amply attested throughout his writings. Sappho's poem is the intertext[56] of Ines' story, of the portrayal of the "unreachable alternation" of her subjectivity.

I have argued that the portrayal of Ines' pain and shame is Gadda's own aggrandizement and awareness of it, but I do not believe it possible to be absolutely certain. What if he untangles the knot he is in by taking his pity and his repentance in the form of abuse, of vengeance?[57] Do we have in Ines just one more instance of woman offered up, displayed to the violence of love and cognition, or its denunciation? In the case of Gadda, we cannot unambiguously conclude whether this is the same old story or the telling of it.

IV Gender Effects

In his notes for a projected novel of 1924, under the heading 'Play *ab interiore*' [Gioco ab interiore] Gadda writes:

> if one accepts the supposition that a true representation *ab interiore* is possible within plurality, what happens then? … The reader must go from inside character number one to inside character number two. In an amorous duet, from inside him to inside her. But the reader together with the author are of one sex. They can intuit the male character, for instance, directly, and the female one only through their male intuition. It follows that they have, of the feminine, an intuition of the intuition… . Perhaps, to ourselves, we seem only male, but in reality, in the mysterious depths of nature, we are simply 'polarized' beings, and 'potentially' we can be one and the other. But this potentiality, which precedes our development, we have forgotten. *Sed latet in imo.* (1983: 89; translation mine; italics mine)

If the (male) author's representation of male subjectivity alone is direct,[58] representing woman "from inside" presents a problem. Since, however, the author is "omnipotent" (1983: 90), it is not an impossible task, though seemingly more complicated. In the *Pasticciaccio*, I believe, Gadda addresses this demand of representation through his usage of gender, gender difference, gender effects.

A knife that is "gloriously drawn out, a nickel-plated, or even silver-plated, spare genital" [estromesso in gloria, come un genitale nichelato, argentato] (89/73), a priest's shoes that priapate like "two forbidden objects" [du affari proibbiti] (182/135): the *Pasticciaccio* presents a wide range of phenomena, from dislocated genitalia to heterologous hens, that I designate *gender effects*. These are the textual effects produced by the author's reflection on gender as difference. There is, in the *Pasticciaccio*, a language of gender that operates within the stories of the characters, an infratext of gender.

These gender effects are not the inflection of inanimate objects by the free-play of an undifferentiated desire, a fluid flux washing identity into polymorphous pleasure and polysemy. I do not propose to find in Gadda a practitioner of "écriture féminine" *avant la lettre*.[59]

Gadda's gender effects work because the valencies male/female are still operative in the discourse of human identity. Without perversity, one might here speak of this as an aspect of Gadda's humanism.

My study suggests the relevance of Gadda's reflection on gender, but does not itself present a theory of gender difference. The distinction between sex and gender as employed in recent theorizations of identity is alien to Gadda, hence in using the term 'gender' rather than 'sex,' I do not mean to affirm for Gadda's textual universe the culture/nature distinction that is the origin of the discussion of gender in contemporary feminist discourse. Gadda concerns himself neither with abstracting the social from the biological nor with collapsing them together again. The characters of the *Pasticciaccio* are men and women, and, while Gadda asks about their difference, he does not question their existence.

Monique Wittig remarks on the notion of the construction of gender in American feminists, of which an example would be Kate Millett's use of gender as sociological category. A nuanced treatment of the claim that gender is not natural, but rather the cultural transformation of the biological is made by Gayle Rubin. Other theories, including Wittig's own, do not operate their critique through a distinction between biological and cultural identity, but Gadda's own identification of sex and gender is obviously precritical.

Why not write here, then, of 'sexual dynamics' or 'sex effects'? First, this terminology fails to suggest the continuities between human and inanimate I wish to trace in Gadda's animation of the world. Second, it fails to evoke the tension of difference carried by 'gender.' Gadda's doubles, slippages, ambiguities take on significance only in the context of the conceptualization of difference.

This category of gender effects can be understood only through the collection and juxtaposition of widely disparate textual phenomena. Thus, what might seem mere 'throw-away' scraps of sexy humor and – what might seem a theme bearing no immediate relation to gender at all – the double, when grouped and examined together, makes obvious those forces at work in the text in relation to which the characters must be read, in relation to which I read Ines. A body part is a part of the character, but also the manifestation of a marking of text, which undermines the character, or, perhaps more accurately, the author's right to write the character.

In the *Pasticciaccio*, the question of representing subjectivity is set in a matrix of constant gender mutation: oscillation, reversal, fault line, double, heterologue. Gender is used by Gadda as the articulation of possibilities, and his text is the proliferation of these possibilities intersecting one another. There are multiplex variations, interlocking series of symbolizations, shifting of attributes at every turn. It is as though there were sex-changes going on constantly. But constant sex-change is an oxymoron. To keep changing, to keep shifting from one sex to the other and back again, is to call into question the idea of sexual identity, and the representation of female subjectivity in this context of constant dislocation, of joker-wild gender marking, finally serves to interrogate all species of difference.

Gadda writes of that "marvelous gadget", a gramophone, that transforms itself "with the most perfect nonchalance, from masculine to feminine and vice versa" [con la più perfetta disinvoltura, di maschio in femmina e viceversa] (212/155), oscillating gender at "whim".

A range of gender reversals twist through the text, male to female, female to male, metamorphosing objects and characters alike, turning persons to genitals and genitals to characters.

A smith, called in by the police to open certain drawers and coffers in Liliana's house, is a "veritable Don Juan of the locks*"[60] [un vero don Giovanni de le serrature]:

> he had a bunch of hooks with an extra little twist in the end, and all he had to do was tickle the lock with one or the other, and it knew at once that it couldn't hold out. With him, locks were like a virtuous woman* who suddenly loses her head.*

> ciaveva un mazzo de rampini co un beccuccio in fonno, e je bastava de faje appena er solletico o coll'uno o coll'antro, che quelle già se sentiveno de nun poté resiste. Pareveno come una donna virtuosa che perde i sensi. (112/88)

At the scene of the theft of the Menegazzi jewels, Signor Bottafavi of the fourth floor, tells of how he chased the thief "with a big revolver, which he chose to display to Doctor Ingravallo" [con un grosso pistolone a revolver: che volle esibire al commissario], and also to the other tenants gathered around: "the women stepped back a pace: 'Well, now don't start shooting at us!" [le donne si fecero un po' indietro: 'Mbè, adesso nun ce spari a noi!']. But they need not fear, for this deadly weapon is not "the same as the kinds crooks have...The ones that really shoot" [come quello de li delinquenti… che spareno sur serio], not, that is, like that of the thief who threatened widow Menegazzi (and who, as it later appears probable, is Enea Retalli). Signor Bottafavi's weapon, after "many years of inactivity" [tanti anni di assoluta inazione], has its safety on. And so he did not "at that moment, try as he might, manage to fire it" [là per là, per quanto avesse tentato, non gli era riuscito di spararlo], because, he says to Ingravallo: "This revolver here, officer, is a gentleman's weapon" [Questo, sor commissario, è er revòrvere d'un galantuomo] (32–3/35).

Among the many bystanders outside the building, at the scene of the crime, a post-man is described on the strength of his "brimming bag" [borsa colma] as being "in a state of advanced pregnancy" [in istato di estrema gravidanza]. The crowd, that "collective pulp" [polpa collettiva], in turn, is surrounded by the "*sui generis* skin" of many bicycle wheels, seemingly impenetrable, until, that is, the policeman Ingravallo "clear[s] a path for himself" [si fece largo] (23/28).

These gender metaphors and reversals bear upon the complex gender placements of Gadda's characters, their positioning in a gender dynamic not defined by biological sex.

Liliana, portrayed otherwise in most classical terms of femininity, in her complicated and roundabout search for progeny, makes many gifts to maids and 'nieces,' and Ingravallo theorizes:

That giving, that donating, that sharing out among others!...: operations, to his way of looking at things, so removed from the carnality and, in consequence, from the psyche of woman... which tends, on the contrary, to take in:[62] to elicit the gift: to accumulate...

Quel dare, quel regalare, quel dividere altrui...: operazioni, a suo modo di vedere, tanto disgiunte dalla carnalità e in conseguenza dalla psiche della donna... che tende vice-versa a introitare: a elicitare il dono: a cumulare... (138/105)

He sees this trait in her as a "sentimental deformation* of the victim" [alterazione sentimentale della vittima] (ibid.), a psychosis, a dissociation. And since Liliana's gifts are to the so-called nieces, or maids, who might produce in their fabulous fecundity a child for her, Ingravallo sees them as a result of sublimated homoeroticism,[63] of a "metaphysical paternity" [una paternità metafisica]. "The God-forsaken woman* ... caresses and kisses in her dreams the fertile womb of her sisters" [La dimenticata da Dio ... accarezza e bacia nel sogno il ventre fecondo delle consorelle] (140/107).

Zamira, otherwise most repellently feminine with her closely described toothless mouth, plays a male role in her training of young men in the scheme of seducing country girls (like Ines), luring them to the city, and then turning them over to prostitution. She plays the male role of mastering her apprentices, both male and female:

She unkierkegaarded little crooks from the province, channeling them 'to work' in the city ... after having purged their souls of any remaining perplexity, or of their last scruples..., she catechized them in the Protection of the Homeless Girl, in competition with the better-known organization of the same name.

Dekirkegaardizava farabutelli di provincia incanalandoli a 'lavorare' in città... dopo avergli deterso l'anima dalle ultime perplessità: o dagli ultimi scrupoli... li catechizzava alla protezione della giovane, in concorrenza con l'omonima società. (202/149)

Conversely, Maresciallo Santarella, the virile law officer of rural Latium, a centaur on his motorbike, is loved and admired in his entire physical glory both by Zamira's so-called niece-apprentices, who dreamed of him "on certain moonlight nights". He is endowed with a most phallically attractive pistol gun, weighing six pounds, whose sight "filled the hearts with joy*" [metteva gioia in core a vederlo] (213/156).[64] And it is not only the female hearts, but those of the petty thieves he catches, as well. These behave like women, "dazzled" by the signs of his authority, by the red stripes of his pants, "by those silver chevrons on his sleeves . . .: by that paunch, by that ass. Yes, ass" [da quei galloni d'argento alla manica . . .: da quella pancetta, da quel culo. Sì, culo] (214/157). With an innate "concupiscence", they surrender themselves to him in a "kind of algolagniac frenzy, of masochist voluptuousness" [sorta di algolagnica frenesia, di voluttà masocona], and let him do with them "whatever he wanted*" [un po' icché voleva] (ibid./156). Yet Santarella, too, is being "revitalized", together with a whole nation, by the "male voice of the Duce" (211/155).[65]

So also the process of winning over male clients for the Standard Oil Company must be for the sales representative a seduction, by virtue of which their resistance is broken down, and their doubts go away, to the point at which they "fall in love* ..., at least a little bit..., *l'espace d'un matin*" [s'innamorino: almeno un tantinello ..., l'espace d'un matin] (105/83). They must be managed as wives would be, and if they cuckold the company, they must be taught a lesson: the great nail of truth must be driven through their heads (108/85).

There are many other examples, among which the Countess Menegazzi who, though there is something "neovirginal" about her, has a "bluish mustache" (25/30); appalled by Liliana's murder, and decrying the waste of her beauty and in equal measure of her dowry, awaiting a justice that will never come, her aunts stand "erect and hard" [ritte e dure] (117/ 91); and even the sun itself, clearly masculine,[66] is at one point "seized with uterine languor: like the ostentatiously handsome hunk* that he is" [preso pure lui da un languore d'utero: ... da quel bellone che è] (288/208); finally, the 'niece' Virginia, dragged to church so that she might mend her ways and stop frightening Liliana with lesbian advances, sings at times in a "sing-song that would have put a baby to sleep" [lagna da fa dormì li pupi], and at times aped "the canons of San Giovanni... with a man's voice" [li canonici de San Giovanni... co la voce d'omo] (186/137).

Fault lines of gender open within the text, like the linkage of the carnal cleft of Liliana's vagina to her slit throat, to the *vagina dedentata*[67] of Zamira's mouth, to the splitting face of dream sorceress Circes, to the black fold ("piega nera") between the brows of Assunta at the end of the novel.[68]

Likewise, the flock of chicken tropes, the *Pasticciaccio*'s chicken calculus, can be read simultaneously as gender effect and exercise of the double-bind power of representation.

I would argue that there are elements introduced into the text that, when interconnected, show their rejection of interconnection. Responding to Riffaterre's terminology in "The Making of the Text" (1985:54–70), I would call these elements of irreducible heterogeneity 'heterologues.' They are not linked homologies, whose contextual dissonance raises them to a plane of re-reading and ultimately of semiotic integration, but equivalences that cannot be made equivalent. One chicken can be related to another, and another to another, and so on, but their analysis gives no textual currency but difference itself.[69]

* * *

The definition of the locus 'woman' by the process of objectification as feminization can be clearly seen in the subplot of the Commendatore Angeloni, who is taken to the police station during the investigation of the Menegazzi robbery, at the beginning of the novel. He is a government clerk of "undoubted morality", but a strangely ambiguous figure, a solitary gourmand, given to the pleasures of admiring Rome's architectural beauty and desiring its edible delicacies:

> He must have been a gourmet, judging at least by the little packages, the truffles…: the kind of package from de luxe grocers, filled with galantine or pâté and tied with a little blue cord.

> Doveva essere un buongustaio: a giudicare almeno dai pacchetti, dai tartufetti…: di quelli dei salumai di lusso, pieni di galantina o di pâté, con il cordino celeste. (42/41)

A sign of his guilt, the commendatore had no wife to cook for him. And so, he lives alone, and attracts Ingravallo's suspicion that he served, no matter how unintentionally, the criminal purposes of the thief (murderer of Liliana?) by apparently befriending a delicatessen delivery boy.

Two sets of thematic and descriptive analogies make explicit Angeloni's positioning as 'woman,' by encoding a double parallelism between him and the two women discussed earlier, Liliana and Ines. Through their persons, Gadda genders his epistemology. To relate Angeloni to them illustrates this epistemology abstracted from sex-identity, thereby placing it in relief.

It is significant here that without a single direct reference, Angeloni emerges as signifying the homosexual male. He is a male, but ambiguous, suspect, open to feminization. Every being-to-be-known will be 'woman,' but Angeloni's homosexuality translates this aspect of his role through the polarities of sex-identity. Angeloni's interrogation proves that a man can be a woman. His homosexuality does not undercut this, rather his positioning as unmanly male reaffirms his narrative function.[70]

Like Liliana, "lost at times in a private dream" [assorta, a volte, in un suo sogno], as she walks "under the shifting clouds of sadness…, [a]t dusk, in that first abandon of the Roman night" [sotto le trasvolanti nubi di tristezza…, (a)ll'imbrunire, in quel primo abbandono della notte romana] (19/26), Angeloni strikes Ingravallo with his sadness, "a kind of reticence in his eyes" [una tristezza…, una tal quale reticenza negli occhi] (41/40).[71] The commendatore belongs to that fraternity of melancholy, "mourning", crow-like clerks that slowly haunt certain "beloved little side streets" [dilette stradicce] around Santa Chiara and the Pantheon, "retracing their steps as if a bit disappointed by the dusk" [sulla via di ritorno… e come un po' delusi del crepuscolo] (42/41).

The sadness Liliana and Angeloni share distances them from others, their secret locates them in the sphere of social pathology.

The analogy is strengthened by Gadda in his 1957 auto-exegetical article on the *Pasticciaccio*, in which he talks about Angeloni: to be melancholy and celibate "in an age that was avid for progeny: an age in which celibacy was classified for contempt" (1958: 114), meant to pay a heavy tax, "almost a shameful fine" (1958: 115), even if "no human or divine law prevents an Italian citizen from loving little artichokes in oil, and from being melancholy and celibate like our Lord... (ibid.; translations mine). Solitary and sterile, the "prosciutófilo" commendatore Angeloni compensates: he brings home sometimes the grocer's packages "with great concern and veneration,* holding them horizontally and on his chest, as if he were nursing them" [con gran riguardo e con ogni venerazione, tenendoli orizzontali e in sul davanti, come desse il latte] (42/41). This transference is even more obvious when, in free indirect discourse, he explains his gluttony:

> He... lived alone. He didn't have any regular tradesmen he dealt with. He bought things here and there: today from one, tomorrow from another. From all the shops in Rome, more or less. A little in each, you might say.... Perhaps only some little pastry, often. Just to satisfy a *whim*... A bit of marinated eel, perhaps, or a spot of galantine.

> Lui... era solo. Non aveva fornitori fissi. Comprava qua e là: oggi da uno e domani da quell'altro. Pe tutte le botteghe de Roma un po'. Un po' per una, se po dì... magari solo quarche pasticcetto, tante vorte. Giusto pe levasse na *svojatura*... Un po' d'anguilla marinata, magari, un po' de galantina. (47/44–5; italics mine)

The term "whim", in Roman dialect *svojatura* and in Standard Italian *svogliatura* (meaning capricious desire, whim), is Belli's. It is related to *scapricciatura*, satisfaction of whim, and specifically refers to " 'delicious and dainty little morsel' to satisfy the 'whims' (*voglie*) of pregnant women".[72] Significantly, Angeloni refuses the sandwich a policeman enthusiastically offers and describes to him, since in those cold, impersonal rooms, the mechanism of the whim does not function: "I don't *feel* like it*; this is the wrong moment" [Non ne ho *voglia*,[73] non è il momento] (44/43; italics mine).

And if, later on, defending his need to have home delivery, Angeloni protests that in his position (but the word used is "condizione"), he could not "go around Rome with a ham on [his] shoulder... with two flasks of wine, one tucked under each arm, looking like a pair of twins, carried by their wet-nurse" [annà in giro pe Roma co un presciutto in collo... co du fiaschi uno de qua uno de là... che pareveno du gemelli in collo a la balia] (52/48), the choice of words still belongs to the discourse of child-bearing.[74]

Andreini writes that "Angeloni is admonished for the same transgression of the invitation to procreate for which Liliana pays with psychological disturbance and death" (123). Like Liliana, he will be sacrificed, and, says Gadda, "of the sacrificed, one must write *ad mortem*".[76] Angeloni will not die, but will become the victim of the same institutional powers faced by Ines.

He is harassed by Ingravallo, "who alternated blandishments and courtesy with rather heavier moods*..., bursts of what seemed sudden impatience..., harsh parentheses" [che alternò blandizie e amabilità varie a fasi un po' più grevi..., scatti come di repentina impazienza..., duri incisi] (45/43). He is brought to exhaustion and physical discomfort. His need to blow his nose signifies weeping, a gesture that is also Ines'. But, when Ingravallo entreats him: "What's troubling you? Tell me. Come, you can confide..." [Che è che ve fa stà male? Ditelo. Su, confidatevi...] (52/48), like Ines, Angeloni resists and will not 'confess': "He insisted he knew nothing, thought nothing, could imagine nothing, concerning that shop assistant" [Sostenne di non saper nulla, di non creder nulla, di non essere in grado di immaginar nulla, di quel fattorino] (46/44).

At one point, Ingravallo himself, though he will not be deterred, perceives in a fit of consciousness/conscience, the horror of Angeloni's suffering. This suffering, like that of Ines, is expressed in terms of the gaze:

alone, seated on a bench in the police station, with upon him all the hairsplitting of the homicide squad..., his eyes brimmed. His poor face, the face of a poor man who wants people *not to look at him...*, his face seemed, to Ingravallo, a mute and desperate protest against the inhumanity, the cruelty of all organized inquisition.*

solo, seduto sur una scranna della questura, con addosso tutte le sofisticherie della squadra mobile..., gli si velarono gli occhi. La sua povera faccia, di poveruomo che desidera *che non lo guardino...*, la sua faccia parve, a Ingravallo, una muta disperata protesta contro la disumanità, la crudeltà d'ogni inquisizione organizzata. (47/44; italics mine)

All he had to do was to disclose, to "explain himself, say what he thought, to talk, sing out, loud and clear. If he thought something, why didn't he spill it?" [spiegarsi, dire quello che pensava, cantare: cantarellare. Se pensava quacche cosa, pecché nun cantava?] (54/49). Exasperating Ingravallo, his melancholy reticence will last out the questioning, his "turns of phrase" will "come to nothing, tapering off, vague and dilatory" [quei rigiri di frasi che non concludevano a nulla e davano soltanto nel vago e nel dilatorio] (53–4/49).

Ingravallo has no actual evidence of guilt, but he subjects Angeloni to an interrogation that finds its model in the inquisition of Ines. Ingravallo treats him as a woman, and actually comforts himself vengefully with the thought that such a virgin reputation as Angeloni has enjoyed will be the victim of his (Ingravallo's) quest for knowledge and of institutional power, a process of deflowering: "Oh, well*... every mother's son is pure as the driven snow... till he has his first fling...with the police" [Mah, ... qualunque figlio 'e bona femmena è illibato, fino al suo primo amore...con la questura].

Even though Ingravallo does not develop an extended personal reflection on Angeloni, by classifying him (as homosexual), he theorizes. For classification is shorthand theorization. The process of labeling is a function of normative nature of social structure, itself a theory. Angeloni has become object, woman, in the course of being looked at, of having to present himself, of being represented.

* * *

I have attempted here to demonstrate the implications of the Gaddian gender effect for his theorization of writing. Provisionally, I have grouped certain gender effects as aids to description, but no final integration is possible, no generalized taxonomy of textual strategies will ensue, since a common denominator for the innumerable and greatly entangled gender effects cannot be found. Gadda struggles against his power as author, a power he has conceived as male.[77] No matter how undifferentiated males and females are in the "mysterious depths of nature", if the intuition mediating representation is male, the representation of female subjectivity is bound to the problematic of representation itself: to make something an object of knowledge is to feminize it, to render it woman. Woman, in this sense, is always the object of knowledge, theory, representation, and the theorizing intelligence, always male. The author and the reader are men talking together, reconstructing woman, creating her, denying her.

V Desire and Differentiation

Fate, Chance and the Double

In his essay "Literary Language and Every-Day Language" [Lingua letteraria e lingua dell'uso], Gadda writes:

> I want the doubles, all of them, by virtue of a mania for possession and a greed for richness: and I want the triples, and the quadruples,[78] even though the Catholic King has not coined them yet: and all the synonyms, used in their various meanings and nuances, of current usage, or of extremely rare usage…. In language, neither the useless nor the too much exists.

> I doppioni li voglio, tutti, per mania di possesso e per cupidigia di richezze: e voglio anche i triploni, e i quadruploni, sebbene il Re Cattolico non li abbia ancora monetati e tutti i sinonimi, usati nelle loro variegate accezioni e sfumature, d'uso corrente, o d'uso rarissimo…. Non esistono il troppo né il vano per una lingua. (1958: 95; translation mine)

Gadda's double is many things.[79]

We shall find in the double a model both of gender polarity and of mimesis, but the double's originary paradigm remains necessarily the self-reflexivity of consciousness itself. Every instance of the double calls forth an association to alter ego. To think is to become another self.

Writing is such a process of self-reflection, and in the measure that self-knowledge is narcissism,[80] Gadda forces proliferation. Greedy for reality, he coins the triples and quadruples, attempting to write his way out of the bind of self-awareness. It is the world he wants to express, the world he wants to get into words.[81]

The grotesque dynamism of ornamentation in these multiples has earned for Gadda the epithet 'baroque.' Gadda himself responded to this, saying, "the world is baroque, and Gadda perceived and portrayed its baroqueness". [82]

Multiplication begins with the double, and the discussion of gender and gender effects is incomplete without a consideration on the theme of the double.

Thus, for the world (and the reproduction of the world) "men: and women" is the primary double and Gadda's theme/motif of the double also is, in all its manifestations, a gender effect, a formulation and reformulation of the question, what is the difference between men and women? the original double, and origin of Gadda's question, what does it mean that a human being is double?[83]

A particular case of narrative and stylistic proliferation, the double presents itself throughout the novel. The *Pasticciaccio*'s plot centers around two crimes that are committed in the same building, the theft of Countess Menegazzi's jewels and Liliana's murder. The palace of the sharp-dealers has two stairways, A and B, with two apartments on each floor. After the crimes, various women living in neighboring buildings play the double number in the Naples lottery (which, by chance, comes out instead in Bari) (86/71), and then go on to play it, banking on the mysterious connection between crime and luck, "at all the best and luckiest" (192) lottery wheels around the nation.

Zamira's workshop/tavern is located at Due Santi (associated by some locals with testicles). There, in this village, can be seen a faded mural of a saintly pair, marked by two strikingly phallic toes.

In Maresciallo Santarella's house there are two plaster cats, both toms, "delivered of a male from Lucca" [partoriti... da un maschio lucchese] (211–12/155). On special assignment to Milan, while pursuing two gentlemen, both of whom are named Salvatore, Santarella buys and brings home a radio with two valves.

Again, Maresciallo Santarella is matched to his subordinate, Brigadiere Pestalozzi (not by chance do these two rural centaurs tend to merge in the reader's mind), and together they form a half of the more important double of historiography. It is through Pestalozzi's reflections that the double historiography is introduced: the urban police, he thinks,

> feed on stories*: in their rivalry with the carabinieri. Each of the two organizations would like to have monopoly on... stories, on History indeed. But History is one alone!

> si ciba appunto di storie: in concorrenza coi carabinieri. Ognuna della due organizzazioni vorrebbe monopolizzare le storie, anzi addirittura la Storia. Ma la Storia è una sola! (198/146)

Nonetheless, "they're capable of hacking it in two:... in a process of detwinning (*degeminazione*) it in two, of amoebic splitting: half for me and half for you" [sono capaci di spaccarla in due: un pezzo per uno: con un processo di degeminazione, di sdoppiamento amebico: metà me metà te] (ibid.). The word "degeminazione" is haunted by its double. Here it means the production of duplicates. The de- intensifies duplication, but morphematically might as well undo it. The amoeba splits in two, but into two ones.

The singleness of History is derogated into a double historiography, it is devolved into psalm and antiphony, it is potted in two contradictory certainties: the police report, the carabiniere report.

L'unicità della Storia si deroga in una doppia storiografia, si devolve in salmo e in antifona, s'invasa in due contrastanti certezze: il rapporto della questura, il rapporto dei carabinieri (199/146)

Then there are the quasi-doubles of the novel, characters whose identities blur, whose specificities seem to dissolve in the tangled threads of the plot. Already introduced are the motorcycle-riding Santarella and Pestalozzi. Two maids, with hypersemanticized names, Virginia and Assunta,[85] become difficult to keep distinct. Two suspected criminals, Enea Retalli and Diomede Lanciani seem, at times, to run together in the narrative.

One technique Gadda employs for such pseudogeminations is the liberal addition of interpretive red herrings. We note that Diomede has a brother Ascanio, who as son of mythic Aeneas connects Diomede and Enea. While the patternings of Roman myth cohere in a general reading, at the level of specific interconnections, these resonances are irrational.[86] The pairing of Diomede and Enea exists for the pairing alone.[87] There are other connections of this kind, ironic and mess-making, and this is really the nature of these blurrings. The so-called nieces/prostitutes of Zamira's "laboratory" (among whom, two cousins, Camilla and Lavinia Mattonari) double the so-called nieces of Liliana Balducci.[88] This use of blurring is continuous with the parallels between characters, such as, among the very many (major or minor), between Ines and Angeloni, Zamira and Liliana.

The double as subtext, again, is the site of closure and non-totalizibility. Because the point about the double is that in it both sameness and difference operate. All genres of duplication, pairs, replications, oppositions thematize a 'metaphysics' of same and different.

Thus, Assunta's dying father, in his own person, evokes the double, hovering at the border between being and non-being, between male and female: "You couldn't understand whether the man was alive or dead: if it was a man or woman" [Non si capiva s'era un vivo o s'era un morto: s'era un omo o una donna] (383/273).

A central and most flagrant example of the double, one that iterates the permeation gender and representation (the other double), and one that symbolizes the frustration of identity, is the dead chicken brought to the police station to stand in for the dead chicken stolen earlier.

In a book filled with chickens and chicken metaphors, this is the first appearance of an actual chicken; its significance is thus emphasized. This first chicken was stolen by the derelict Ines from a woman vendor in Piazza Vittoria. She, "to enlighten the police", brings to the station "a sample chicken…, in every way similar to its colleague which had vanished from sight three days before" [un pollo-campione…, simile in tutto al collega resosi irreperibile tre giorni prima] (196/145). There is an absolute literalism in proposing to represent one dead chicken by another,[89] and there is this representation's complete failure, since it is not the same chicken.

Again, Gadda's gluttony makes for an added pleasure – yet another example of failure of identity: at the police station, a pair of shoes is also provided by another woman vendor to represent the pair stolen with the chicken by Ines: they are both lefts![90]

Analeptically, the reader finds in this incident the closing of Gadda's meditation on representation begun with Ines. This last set of doubles links then again the problematic of representation to that of gender, specifically, to that of the difference of woman.

Gadda's representation of the unrepresentability of women's integrity as desiring subjects inscribes his own resistance to the setting up of difference between men and women.

Liliana Balducci is dead, Ingravallo's idea of Liliana is dead, and Gadda's own work, his doubling of the world, an impossibility, because there is no doubling, only the double, the triple, the quadruple, and so on into a mess of threads and differences.

Homoerotics: The Failure of the Same

Ingravallo, for whom women are excluded, is juxtaposed not only to Santarella surrounded by women: with her *groviglio*[91] of maids and nieces, Liliana also confronts the detective, to form with him a deeper double as counterpart in the theme of homoerotic love.[92]

Analyzing the peculiar circumstances in which Liliana has set herself, Ingravallo concludes that here manifests a type of homosexuality. He conceives this as a 'metaphysical paternity', that is, in a classic male interpretation of female homosexuality, he sees in her a man.[93]

The parallels between Liliana and Angeloni have already been discussed. Full of innuendo, Detective Ingravallo clearly regards Angeloni as homosexual, but never uses the term. He categorizes without explicitly denominating.

That the novel's author represents himself in Angeloni and in Ingravallo is a critical commonplace. It would seem that this equivalence is transitive, the identifications yielding, through Gadda,[94] a homosexual Ingravallo.

"Cherchez la femme", the detective's injunction, involves the finding of woman even where you do not want to find one – "ch'i femmene se retroveno addó n'i vuò truvà" (6/17) – in a man, in oneself.[95]

Ingravallo finds a man in Liliana, but worse, does he find a woman in himself?

There is considerable textual support for Ingravallo's latent homosexuality. At the murder scene, for example, Ingravallo reacts to the exposed Liliana by associating her mound/cleft to Michelangelo's statues of Dawn and Dusk in the chapel of San Lorenzo, feminine figures whose genitalia were not represented by the artist:

> … the gentle softness of that mount,* … that central line, the carnal mark of
> the mystery… the one that Michelangelo (Don Ciccio mentally saw again his
> great work, at San Lorenzo) had thought it wisest to omit".

... la dolce mollezza del monte, ...quella riga, il segno carnale del mistero...
quella che Michelangelo (don Ciccio ne rivide la fatica, a San Lorenzo) aveva
creduto opportuno di dover omettere. (68/59)

The association reiterates the theme of "women excluded". Michelangelo, famous
homosexual, deletes the "mark" of the feminine.

This absence of female genitalia in Michelangelo's statues corresponds to the phalli-
cism of the huge toe of Saint Joseph in his painting of the Holy Family around which
Gadda develops a most interesting theory of light and (pro)creation.

In the same passage, the double town Due Santi is site of a mural of Peter and Paul, a
pair of men. And this mural is notable for the depiction of the saints' respective toes: "The
two haughty digits... were projected, hurled forward: they traveled on their own: they
almost, paired off as they were, stuck in your eye: indeed, into both your eyes" [I due dit-
toni insuperbiti... si proiettavano, si scagliavano in avanti: viaggiavano per conto loro: ti
davano, così appaiati, dentro un ochhio, a momenti: anzi, dentro a tutt'e due] (272/196).
The very act of painting the toes is described by Gadda in the language of ejaculation.[96]

Ingravallo responds to the voluptuous Assunta and other maids or nieces. He is jealous of men successful with women. In his portrayal, there are no explicit homosexual
traits. *Sed latet in imo.* Unexpressed, suggested by a pattern of associations, Ingravallo's
homosexuality is, in the technical sense, latent. Latent in the text, it is brought to awareness only by the linkages.

Ingravallo and Liliana are both childless. The sterile loves of Liliana define the economy of the same that characterizes Ingravallo's epistemic failure. Feminizing the other, he
is left only with the male/same, but this can only finally mean that he is left alone in the
solipsism of unconsummated desire.

Zamira, *Femme Fatale*

Just as the discussion on gender must consider the doubles of the story, so the discussion
of the double cannot but involve an examination of the theme of chance and fate. The
whole of the *Pasticciaccio* may be seen as a meditation on chance and fate. All around the
nation, people play the lottery with the double number (86/71).

The lottery symbolizes chance. It is chance that resolves the investigation of the jew-
elry theft. Not a case, Gadda remarks, of "non datur casus, non datur saltus" (256/1185).
And the idea of the double number is related by Gadda to that of chance.[97]

In this context, the character Zamira might be seen to embody Gadda's meditation on
the play of lived and mortal time: "the days and events seemed to orbit around her, to rise
and vanish in her" [i giorni e i casi parevano orbitare d'attorno a lei, sorgere e vanire da
lei] (203/149).

At once powerful and powerless, she appears as a Fate, expert in occult arts, but common, repulsive, a Fate trying to make ends meet. Zamira is a diplomate in fortune-telling

and the crafts she plies all suggest her magical powers.

Her country brothel is a tavern where, Circe-like, she offers potions to carabinieri. It is also a dying-mending shop, the dying cauldron like that of Beelzebub, her patron (193). Zamira is described as "teacher of sewing and not of sewing" [maestra de sarta e non de sarta] (200/147). This title, of course, suggests the other less reputable arts of which she is instructress, but more, its disjunction spreads before us all the world's possibilities.[98] The disjunction is exhaustive.

> There was everything you could want. A place, in short, this workshop of Zamira's whose like you would never find, still less its better, for distilling a drop, a single and splendid drop of the eternally prohibited or eternally unlikely Probability.

> Tutto quello che ce voleva, c'era. Un luogo, insomma, il laboratorio della Zamira, da non si poter incontrare il più opportuno a distillarvi una goccia, una goccia sola e splendida della eternamente proibita o eternamente inverisimile Probabilità. (206/139)

In her workshop time is woven. The Fates are weavers. Gadda writes of the "flashing shuttle" of thought [saettata spola], of the "warp of furtive glances" [ordito degli sguardi furtivi] (209/154).

Zamira's first mention in the text stresses the spelling of her name which in its last and initial letters expresses the full range of possibility:

> …a certain Pàcori, Pàcori Zamira. Z like in Zara, A like in Ancona! Zamìra! that's right. Za-Mir-a! known to many, if not all, in the area of Marino and Albano for many of her merits: if not for all of them.

> …certa Pàcori, Pàcori Zamira. Zamira! Zeta come Zara, a come Ancona! Zamìra! …sì, sì, Zamìra! nota a molti, se non a tutti, in quel di Marino e di Albano, per i molti suoi meriti: se non per tutti i suoi meriti. (189/14o)

Zamira evokes the compossible (207/152) and invokes the devil (209/153). When the carabinieri leave without arresting her, this is ascribed to the grace of "il cavalier Forcella", Old Nick, (298/214), who has heard her prayers. Descriptions of Zamira iterate this demonic connection. Her face is lit with the fires of Beelzebub's mint (243/176), the devil is in her head (297/214).

As witch, Zamira has a special function in Gadda's treatment of the feminine. Magic, Gadda's text makes clear, is related to the feminine. And the sensitivity of women, their "ovaricity" (170/127) can be tied, I think, to the "uterus in us" (297/213), that is, in all human beings, which is a subratiocinative power of consciousness that recognizes and fears the magical, an irrational intelligence (the uterus in us is "a reasonable one"

[170/127]), that reacts to the "unreason of the powers of darkness" (296/213).

Thus does Pestalozzi, for all his male pride in rationality, instruct Zamira to keep her fingers still, for she is working a spell, like the "witch-doctors" described by Gadda in ugly, mocking terms. But women are especially tied to this ovaricious intelligence, they who suffer "headache in the belly" [Er mal di testa, noi donne, ce l'abbiamo qua] (283/204), according to the periodicity of moons. Zamira's attempt to deflect Pestalozzi's interrogation by bringing in her nieces' 'monthlies' can be read as a magical use of menstrual blood, traditionally a taboo substance.

Zamira is described as a "bellona",[99] an ostentatious, vulgar beauty and "sorceress" (277/200). Identified with Circe by her potion-serving profession, she appears, merged with the countess, as Circe in Pestalozzi's erotic dream (265–9/193–5). Like "a Teresa repossessed by the devil" (268/194), Circe opens to ecstasy, her face splitting open like a watermelon, linking her to the toothless mouth of Zamira, and to the slit throat of Liliana.

Zamira is witch-like in her strange, sometimes youthful, sometimes wrinkled, appearance and has a perverse allure for some of the clients with her toothless mouth, which, "opened badly, like a hole, to speak: worse, it stretched at the corners into a dark and lascivious smile" [viscida e salivosa… si apriva male e quasi a buco a parlare: peggio, si stirava agli angoli in un sorriso buio e lascivo] (200/147).

This moist cavity, Gadda repeatedly describes in terms that call up at once repulsion and fascination. Zamira's mouth is a red, feverish hole, bubbling with fluids: "[c]onsiderable saliva lubricated the outburst of her speech" [(a)lquanta saliva le lubrificava la scaturigine del discorso] (208/153). In short, it is a *vagina dedentata*. The vagina dentata is a projection of male castration anxiety. Can Zamira's mouth, detoothed, then present itself as an authentic vagina? Her gums, "deprived of the cutting edge of the former ivory, seemed today the entrance, the free ante-chamber of every amorous magic" [sguerniti d'ogni taglio dell'antico ivorio, parevano oggimai la soglia, la libera anticamera d'ogni amorosa magia] (208/153). There is no question that this symbolism is fully intended by Gadda. A vagina without teeth cannot castrate by biting, but it can swallow maleness, it can ensorcelle and put to sleep ("ammammolare"). And this too would seem to be a form of castration.[100]

The work of Circe is to render the male drowsy, to make the male the mother's baby, to return the devil to the womb. The Circean territory is precisely that of the most exalted level of male potential, from which Ingravallo had been excluded by the English erotologist (241/175).

Against the more usual meaning of *femme fatale*, Zamira truly is one, linking the feminine with fate.

Canny Love

Zamira is not only mistress of the occult arts but also medium for training in crime. "She

unkierkegaarded little crooks of the province, channeling them 'to work' in the city"
[Dekirkegaardizava farabutelli di provincia incanalandoli a 'lavorare' in città...]
(202/149). Madam of a country brothel, she is specifically instructress in the art of "canny
love" [amore avveduto]. Ines tells her interrogators of this, describing Zamira's relations
with Diomede. Zamira advises Diomede, says Ines,

'about how to make us girls fall for him without him falling for any of us.' A
code, an etiquette of canny love: an initiation to controlled, bookkept gallantry, if not even to profitable gallantry... profitable for both, 'for him and for
her:' her, Zamira.

'de fa girà er boccino a noi antre regazze, senza fasse arubbà er core da
nissuna.' Un codice, o un galateo, dell'amore avveduto: una iniziazione alla
galanteria controllata, contabilizzata, se non proprio alle galanterie
profittevoli... profittevoli pe tutt'e due, 'pe lui e pe lei': lei Zamira. (244/177)

This "canny love", the "profitable gallantry" in which Zamira catechizes her young
crooks is possible because

...the poor creatures of the weaker sex asked for nothing better... than to lean
on someone, to attach themselves to something, that would be able to share
with them a forgetful orgasm,*[101] the sweet pain of living... .

...le deboli creature del sesso non attendevano di meglio... se non appoggiarsi
a un qualcuno, d'attaccarsi a un qualche cosa, che fosse buono a divider seco
un immemore orgasmo, la dolce pena del vivere... . (202/149)

There is, it may be argued, also a feminine version of "canny love" instanced by the
dowry-extracting attentions of one of Liliana's wards, Ines.
I believe that this "amore avveduto" must be compared to the courtly passion of
Ingravallo for Liliana. They are counterparts, a debased and an elevated love, both of
which are failures of any real relation. Each involves a discrepancy of view between 'part-
ners.' It could be argued that there are no real relationships in *Pasticciaccio* at all. Neither
canny nor courtly love gives a relation.[102] Each of the characters is intermeshed with others, but no relationship has reality, presence, in the book. Each character spins his
world.[103]
It might be noted here that, while Ingravallo's sublimated love functions as an aspect
of his social displacement, this comparison/ contrast between canny and courtly love cannot be assimilated to a class distinction. Giuliano Valdarena, Liliana's cousin, in his own
bourgeois fashion, does practice an "amore avveduto" not so different in spirit from
Diomede's (and not only with women, also with the clients of his firm). Ingravallo calls
Valdarena "a handsome crook" (160/120), and his reaction to both men is identical.

Zamira, while teaching Diomede the ways of pimping, pays him to have sex with her:

> He had granted her the best, or the worst, of his own spirit of initiative…. [H]e had boldly insuflated it, into the sorceress: perhaps, in fact certainly, after suitable remuneration. 'Because he didn't have any cash before,' Ines blurted, 'and then he had some.'

> Le aveva conceduto il meglio, o il peggio, del proprio spirito d'iniziativa…. [G]lie lo aveva audacemente insufflato, alla maga: forse, anzi di certo, dietro adeguata remunerazioncella. 'Visto che prima nun ce l'aveva, le rùzziche,' scappò detto alla Ines, 'poi ce l'aveva.' (246/178)

Liliana is, in some sense, trying to buy her cousin. A chaste and virtuous wife (13/22), Liliana does not purchase from Giuliano, Ingravallo thinks, the one thing most suited to her purpose:

> To Ingravallo, there came in a flash, between his grief and his contempt, that it was much more natural and much simpler, something very logical, since it really meant so much to Liliana, this baby, that instead of giving him, this handsome crook here…, the gold chains of the dead… babies… from chains of gold don't come, surely… it was much quicker if she had made him give her, instead, another little plaything, much more suited to the purpose.

> A Ingravallo gli balenò, tra il dolore e lo sdegno, ch'era molto più naturale e molto più semplice, una cosa molto più logica, postoché davvero Liliana ci teneva tanto, a un bambino, che invece di regalargli lei, a quel bel guappo lì…, le catene d'oro dei morti… bambini, dalle catene d'oro, non ne vien fuori di sicuro… era molto più presto fatto se si faceva regalare lei, da lui, invece, un qualche altro ninnolo un po' più adatto allo scopo. (160/120)

The description of Ingravallo's reaction to the story of Valdarena suggests that Ingravallo the psychologist is even more repelled by the symbolic status of Liliana's futile acts, than he might have been by the act itself.

Yet love savvy and sublime cannot be fully assimilated one to the other. In neither do the lovers come together in understanding, but these loves differ in that "amore avveduto", wised-up love, achieves its aim. Small and mean-spirited, it brings profit, it brings satisfaction. This is possible, because of the reduction it operates upon the world.

Ingravallo's sublimated love also operates a reduction of sorts, reducing the living subjectivity of Liliana to his idea of her, but by virtue of continual displacement, it remains frustrated. Ingravallo's story of Liliana is born of frustration and never escapes it. This story, this love, is rather the elaboration of the distance between theory and the 'object' of theory. The theory, the story, generates Ingravallo's own subjectivity. The stories told by the betrayed, prostitute Ines and seamstress Lavinia, are versions of this constitution of subjectivity.

Moral judgment may be passed on a love that traffics in betrayal, but in itself it does not exist at the level of morality. The other love, while no truer, has through the powers of displacement moved into the realm of moral possibility, for in the interstice between desire and satisfaction is openness to the world. It yields subjectivity not cut off from the world, but open to the wounds of perception. Frustration is source of the lie, the fable, but these themselves may become the medium of contact with reality.

VI Gadda's *Praticaccia*

Ingravallo "repents" his pronouncement on women, "afraid of having said too much":

> ...he used to say, but this a bit wearily, 'you're sure to find skirts where you don't want to find them.' A belated Italian revision of the trite 'cherchez la femme.' And then he seemed to repent, as if he had slandered the ladies, and wanted to change his mind. But that would have got him into difficulties. So he would remain silent and pensive, afraid he had said too much.

> ...soleva dire, ma questo un po' stancamente, 'ch'i femmene se retroveno addó n'i vuò truvà.' Una tarda riedizione italica del vieto 'cherchez la femme.' E poi pareva pentirsi, come d'aver calunniato 'e femmene, e voler mutare idea. Ma allora si sarebbe andati nel difficile. Sicché taceva pensieroso, come temendo d'aver detto troppo. (6/17)

How much was "too much", how much more than a bit of difference would warrant? And is not the "quantum of eros" (which generates the crime, as Ingravallo believes), the "quantum" of "fantasia" of thinker or writer (which generates the theory, the narrative), necessarily an excess?

For himself, Gadda declares[104] that he does not belong to "any pruning fraternity". "It may be", he says, "that the mania for order coerces some people to prune the tree of all the whimsical branches of liberality and luxury".[105] This "mania for order" defines a usage described by Gadda as "petty bourgeois", a usage that cannot for him become law. "I repudiate", he writes, "such obligation and such law". For, though "humour, cheerfulness, anger, tangles,[106] lies, fraud, move men to abuse language and pen", though these causes bring about "moral abuse", they also allow *"full linguistic usage"* (1958: 98–99; translation mine; italics mine). Fulfillment of linguistic play per force brings about moral abuse, but moral abuse is not failure, it is excess.

A Mess of Details

This study suggests that there is a type of humanism in Gadda concerned with gender difference, that Gadda experiences the problem of gender difference as having an ethical dimension, and ties this problematic to his ethics of representation. Nevertheless, the very evidence of this claim, my analysis of his difficulties with the representation of woman's subjectivity, is also evidence of Gadda's deep horror at the occult nature of female sexuality.[107] He identifies the living subjectivity of woman with her dead body. This is the site of struggle, but also, I believe, of his defeat. The female "non confiteor" is not for Gadda only living resistance to representation, it is also death. It is impossible here, especially for the reader of Gadda's *Cognizione* with its tormented mother/son relationship, ending in the mother's brutal beating, not to be put in mind of Simone de Beauvoir's interpretation of the Oedipus complex as male anxiety of differentiation from the mother's body as matrix of matter, involving the identification of that body with the fate of decay, putrefaction, death (220–22).[108]

If we return to the beginning of Ingravallo's investigations into Liliana's life, we find (part of Don Corpi's account of the series of maids/ nieces) an excursus that reflects a basic ambivalence towards women I ultimately judge to be the author's.

Liliana's second ward, Ines (not the prostitute, but her 'double'), stimulated into a natural response by Liliana's tenderness, one day decides that " 'she wanted to follow her vocation' " ['voleva seguire la sua vocazione'], to get married, that is. Exhibiting the right proportion of foresight and determination, ward Ines successfully extracts "a bit of dowry, …a trousseau,*" from "the daughterly and urban, adventure" [un po' di dote,... un corredo; (d)all'avventura filiale, e urbana]. In her systematic premeditation "of every gesture or smile or word or whim or glance or kiss" [d'ogni proprio gesto o sorriso o parola o frullo, o sguardo o bacio], she manifests that "tacit will of woman" [tacito volere della donna], who, Gadda elaborates, is

> past mistress, on occasion, in prompting the thought without even giving its outline verbally: with hints, lateral tries and counter tries, mute waiting: setting off a process of induction…: with the same technique whereby she is wont to surround and protect (and direct towards the Good*) the first stumbling steps of a little boy*:[109] channeling it, however, where she wants, which is where he can wee-wee in the most seemly way, and with utter relaxation.

> maestra, a volte, nel suggerire un'idea senza neppur disegnare verbalmente il contorno: per accenni, per prove e controprove laterali, per mute attese: dandole un'avvio d'induzione…: con la stessa tecnica onde suol circondare e proteggere (e dirizzare al bene) i primi passi al primo barcollare d'un parvolo: incanalandolo però dove vuol lei, che è dove lui potrà far pipì nei modi più dicevoli, e con rilasciamento esauriente. (180/133)

This, I believe, serves as modifier to the story of Ingravallo's sublimation, with its underlying dynamic of instinctual desire. In the light of the excursus, the "dreamed architectures", the harmonious order established by Liliana's noble gaze turns out to be precisely this kind of female "channeling",[110] or prompting, of male thought. It is important to remember that when he wrote his sonnet for Liliana, "he couldn't make all the rhymes come out right" [non gli eran venute tutte le rime] (91/74). This failure can be read as emblem of the frustration implicit in a sublimated eros.

It comes as no surprise, then, that an analysis of the sequence of descriptions of Liliana's dead body, as seen by Ingravallo, yields not a pure emotion, but something more messy, more debased. The policeman's fascination contains, yes, pity and love, but in equal measure hostility and repulsion.

In the space of one chapter, five passages focus on the corpse. They share lexical and thematic variations that will converge in the same semiosis.

The first comes at the beginning of the chapter, and begins the scene-of-the-crime episode. From the body, that horrible thing, the description moves to its clothes, by virtue of propinquity: from the skirt thrown back to reveal the white, immaculate underpants, to the lilac-coloured garters which form a bridge from the embroidered edge of the underpants to the silk-stockings, over a strip of bare flesh of "chlorotic pallor" [pallore da clorosi] (68/58). Liliana's clothes in their distinction, but especially the garters, mentioned twice, bring an association with class. Their hue "seemed to give off a perfume, to signify at the same time the frail gentleness both of the woman, and of her station" [dare un profumo, significava a momenti la frale gentilezza e della donna e del ceto]. But the elegance of her clothing is now "extinguished", spent, as is that of "her actions,* the secret manner of her submission" [degli atti, il secreto modo della sommissione] (ibid./59).

In a first transformation, Liliana seems to be reduced by death to the specificity of her attraction as woman. Class, as it were, evaporates, to leave flesh:

The precise work of the knitting, to the eyes of those men used to frequenting maidservants, shaped uselessly the weary proposals of a voluptuousness whose ardor, whose shudder, seemed to have barely been exhaled from the gentle softness of that mount,* from that central line, the carnal mark of the mystery... the one that Michelangelo (Don Ciccio mentally saw again his great work, at San Lorenzo) had thought it wisest to omit.[112]

L'esatto officiare del punto a maglia, per lo sguardo di quei frequentatori di domestiche, modellò inutilmente le stanche proposte d'una voluttà il cui ardore, il cui fremito, pareva essersi appena esalato dalla dolce mollezza del monte, da quella riga, il segno carnale del mistero... quella che Michelangelo (don Ciccio ne rivide la fatica, a San Lorenzo) aveva creduto opportuno di dover omettere. (ibid.)

Impatient with this undesired but most meaningful reflection, Ingravallo ends by rejecting it. In a text that abounds in ostensibly realistic detail, we see him exclaim: "Details! Forget it!* [Pignolerie! Lassa perde!].[113]

In the same register with the ekphrasis, to be noted here, is the elevated language in which Liliana's sex is mentioned, "the carnal mark of mystery", which is itself in tension with the use of the colloquial /dialectal "Lassa perde!" ("Forget it!").

Another passage repeats the same mode of translating the body, but is one in which a language of philosophical reflection replaces that of art:

> death seemed to Don Ciccio an extreme decompounding of possibles... [l]ike the dissolving of a unity which cannot hold out any longer, the sudden collapse of relationships, of all ties with organizing reality.

> la morte gli apparve, a don Ciccio, decombinazione estrema dei possibili... [c]ome il risolversi d'una unità che non ce la fa più ad essere e ad operare come tale, nella caduta improvvisa dei rapporti, d'ogni rapporto con la realtà sistematrice. (84/70)

In both passages the motif of weariness is at work, as indeed it is throughout the chapter (its role being, I believe, to bring home the specificity of the dead body, almost a conceit of the decomposition of the body): the "weary proposals of voluptuousness" of the first segment becomes the syntagm "cannot hold out any longer", and the "tired periwinkle" [stanca pervinca] of the face in the second.[114]

From this level of abstraction, as if to counteract it, comes the notation of a concomitant state in Ingravallo: "Shudders ran down his spine... .He was sweating again" [Dei brividi gli la schiena... .Sudava]. Not intellect, but emotion, a panic, one might say, at having evoked the destroyed "tender flower of the being, of the soul" [tenero fiore della persona e dell'anima] (84–5/ibid.). Apparently dissimilar, this too links the two texts: whereby Ingravallo's shivers and sweating are the equivalent of his earlier impatience at the idea of Michelangelo's omission. Both these reactions counteract his tendency to abstraction.

Another section (which in the chapter comes second) powerfully reinforces Ingravallo's positioning in relation to his colleagues and subordinates. He observes that "the underpants weren't bloodied; they left uncovered two patches of thigh, two rings of flesh: down to the stockings, glistening blond skin" [le mutandine nun ereno insanguinate: lasciavano scoperti li du tratti de le cosce, come du anelli de pelle: fino a le calze, d'un biondo lucido] (70/60). And since, "thought will not be prevented: it arrives first", and you cannot "erase from the night the flash of an idea: of an idea slightly dirty" [non si può impedire il pensiero: arriva prima lui. Non si può scancellare dalla notte il baleno d'un'idea: d'un'idea un poco sporca] (159/120), Ingravallo goes on:

> The furrow of the sex... it was like being at Ostia in the summer, or at Forte dei Marmi of Viareggio, when the girls are lying on the sand baking themselves, when they let you glimpse whatever they want. With those tight jerseys they wear nowadays.

> La solcatura del sesso... pareva d'esse a Ostia d'estate, o ar Forte de marmo de

52

Viareggio, quanno so' sdraiate su la rena a cocese, che te fanno vede tutto quello che vonno. Co quele maje tirate tirate d'oggigiorno. (70/60)

The vulgarity of the image also equates Liliana herself with common women, maids perhaps, from which in life she had been distanced.

Immediately before Ingravallo's reflection on death and the decomposing of possibles, in fact the very beginning of the sentence that issues in this reflection iterates the contemplation of a dead Liliana:

> that body of a woman... no longer possessed modesty or memory... .In the obscenity of that involuntary pose – whose motives... were the skirt lifted back by* the outrage, the parted legs, and above them, the swell and furrow of voluptuousness... inflamed the weak.

> quer corpo de donna... nun ciaveva più pudore né memoria... .Nella turpitudine di quell' atteggiamento involontario-della quale erano motivi... e la gonna rilevata addietro dall'oltraggio e l'ostensione delle gambe, su su, e del rilievo e della solcatura... incupidiva i più deboli. (84/69)

The "furrow of the sex", all too visible, is no worse than the "furrow of voluptuousness" that provokes lust in the weak, and once again Ingravallo is one of them. Thus the "carnal mark of mystery" which Michelangelo did well not to represent is now no more than the common flesh of common women.

In death, Liliana is increasingly debased, and with her, Ingravallo, too, is brought back (temporarily, but also absolutely) to his own class level.

Ingravallo suffers for Liliana and because of her.[115] His reactions to the dead woman form a terrible knot: his desire, his debasement, his horror, his anguish, his fury. Each runs into its apparent opposite. Thus, for Ingravallo the compelling horror of Liliana's body, which had preserved at first a certain nobility, had remained a being and in which subjectivity seemed still present even if only as tepid memory, forces the full reification that renders that body a "poor encumbrance" [povero ingombro] (86/71). All his powers of intellect reach in anguished empathy to affirm the subjectivity, the living consciousness, of his lost love, to animate her, but this animation is necessarily only the soul that was granted to women by the Council of Mainz in 589 A.D. Reaching out to her, he recreates her, he creates her, and makes her objectification complete.

As he proceeds with the routine gathering of forensic evidence, Ingravallo oscillates between outraged tenderness for the lady who had configured his desire, and hence defined him, and outraged fury at Liliana herself for her reduction to mere female flesh, diminishing him in obliterating a primary index of his self-differentiation.

The last meditation on the body reads:

> ...those eyes, the horrible wound..., [t]hat skirt... thrown back like that, as if

by a gust of wind: a hot, greedy gust, blowing from Hell. Summoned by a rage, by such contempt, only the gates of Hell could have granted it passage.

> …quegli occhi, la orrenda ferita…, (q)uella gonna… così buttata addietro, come da un colpo di vento: una vampa calda, vorace, avventatasi fuori dall'inferno. Chiamata da una rabbia, da uno spregio simile, erano le porte d'Inferno che le avevano dovuto dar passo. (86/71)

Relating this metaphorical conjecture to his unremitting theory of eros in crime (but plying also a journalistic stereotype), Ingravallo thinks this "a crime of passion" [delitto passionale] (ibid.).

As to specific motives, he asks himself, "Rape? Desire? Vengeance?" [Oltraggio? Brama? Vendetta?]. The whole mess of causes is here, and they are all equal in producing the mess, the *pasticcio*, not only of crime, but of woman. The rage and contempt that killed might be those of the criminal, against life, against women, against this woman in particular. But they are also Ingravallo's, now, for his debased Madonna. How appropriate then that he should remark, at a later point of the investigation, that

> what was important to him…, was, above all, the face, the attitude…, of the spectators and the protagonists of the drama: of this bunch of swindlers* and sonsabitches that people the world, and their gossiping* women, fucking madams* and sows.

> [q]uello che je premeva…, era più de tutto la faccia, il contegno…, degli spettatori e de li prottagonisti der dramma: de sto branco de fregoni e fiji de mignotte che stanno ar monno, e de le commare loro e madame porche futtute. (112/88)

And this rage and this contempt is Gadda's as well, who, "pasticciando di tutto" in his representation of women (and men), must regard his own art as proliferating mess of details, contradictory, pedantic, hairsplitting, causing impatience and shame. Yet, given Gadda's conceptualization of reality and representation, it is unavoidable mess.

*　*　*

Liliana's throat wound operates the integration of two equivalences. First, it stands for the untouched "furrow" of her sex; she was not raped, there was no bloodshed there. The wound is described as open, with jagged edges. It is the locus of penetration.[116]

Second, with its "red strands, like thongs", its "black foam of the blood, clotted already", with its "tiny bubbles still in the midst", this wound is assimilated to Zamira's mouth, which stands itself for vagina. Thus since the wound/mouth is not a real vagina, Liliana is both raped and impenetrable. The wounding movement of the knife that violated will not fecundate. The blood that should have come at childbirth came instead at death, displaced. Behind it, Liliana remains untouchable, closed.

Further, it is this blood as taboo, (as murder is taboo), that is described as *pasticcio*, mess, twice in the description of the detective's reconstruction of the murder.

The Menegazzi theft is also called *pasticcio*. This nominal identity draws the interdiction, the taboo, from the level of the plot, to the meta-narrative title of the novel, the *pasticciaccio*. Ingravallo's *pasticcio* of Liliana's resistance in death is also the *pasticcio* of representing female subjectivity, it is Gadda's text. Ingravallo, who cannot ignore, as did Michelangelo, the issue of sex, yet is denied entry, is paralleled by Gadda who has to make it central, has to write the *pasticcio* at another power, as *pasticciaccio*.

The Dream of the *Pasticciaccio*: Gadda's Run-Away *Mise-En-Abyme*

Gadda recounts at length Brigadiere Pestalozzi's dream of a topaz, which becomes a sub-text[117] in the narrative.

Riding his bike in the early morning, hoping to recover – at Zamira's 'laboratory' – the Countess Menegazzi's jewels, in particular her topaz, the memory of a perplexing, "endless dream of the night" [l'interminabile sogno della notte] is brought to Pestalozzi's mind: "he had seen in his sleep, or had dreamed... what the hell had he managed to dream of?... a strange being, a mad being*: a top-ass.[118] He had dreamed of a topaz..." [(a)veva veduto nel sonno, o sognato...che diavolo era stato capace di sognare?... uno strano essere: un pazzo: un topazzo. Aveva sognato un topazio] (265/192).

A series of metamorphoses begins. To Pestalozzi's– but also Gadda's – question, "what is, after all, a topaz?" [che cos'è, infine, un topazio?], a dictionary-like definition is given: "a faceted glass" [un vetro sfaccettato]. From this, the strange being becomes a lamp, or lantern, "un fanale giallo giallo", a very yellow lamp, which grows, gets larger with every moment, changing itself again into a sunflower, and then into "a malignant disk" [un disco maligno] (265/192). As the brigadiere rides (for in the dream he is on his bike, following the topaz, as on the morning after when he recalls it), this disk escapes his wheels, "rolling forward..., by force of* mute magic" [rotolando inanzi... per muta magia] (266/192).

The "broken-and-entered and detopazed" [la domicilioaggredita e detopaziata] Menegazzi (257/185), called here interchangeably "marchessa" and "contessa", appears in the dream drunk and screaming obscenities, complaining that the brigadieri "weren't bright enough to overtake on any road, or path, the damned* topaz, the awful yellow* thing" [non erano buoni a raggiungerlo su nessuna strada o stradazia, il topazio maledetto, il giallazio] (266/192). At Casal Bruciato, where Camilla Mattonari will turn out to live, on the road to the bridge of the Divino Amore, the malignant disk/sunflower changes yet again into a big, awful, rat: a "topaccio". [119]

This creature takes to the railroad, pursued now by the Rome-Naples express (as transformation of the speeding brigadiere), "after the sunset... almost already into the

Circean darkness". About to be run over, it goes off the tracks, to the fields and the swamps, anticipating the derailment of the pursuing train. Women signal-keepers calling the topaz mad, shout that it must be stopped.

It is the "Circean" quality of time/territory that will perform the transformation of la Menegazzi into the "contessa Circia" who is now presiding at an orgiastic merry-making at her "Castel Porcano" by the sea. She, a sorceress, orders a phial for sleep, for "the dream of not being" [(d)el sogno di non essere], to be given to the "imminent pigs" (later called satyrs) that are already attracted by the scent of her "(perpetually) open snuffbox" [tabacchiera in apertura (perpetua)] (267/193).

Nereids, also called "pupils" [alunne], having come out of the waves, naked, dance a fantastic mating *sicinnis*, a "mammary ritual", that is "falsely apotropaic".[120] The crazed rat interrupts it, falling, suddenly multiple, between their legs. Some of the frightened beauties, "forgetting their nakedness" [smemoratesi d'essere nude], try to pull down their skirts, "to protect a defenseless delicacy: but the skirts were only a dream. And so was their delicacy" [a proteggere una delicatezza indifesa: ma la gonna se la sognaveno. E la delicatezza artrettanto] (268/193–94). Some flee into the swamps, into the thicket [macchia] of ilexes, and some, "poetesses and sea-creatures, diving from the lunar rocks of the circeum" [poetesse ed oceanine precipiti da le scogliere lunari del circeo], plunge into the sea foam.

The countess, whose mouth splits open into a cleft [fenditura], like "the watermelon after the first incision" [il cocomero dopo la prima incisione] (268/194), invokes the devil, who turns out to be instead an impotent Mussolini, "the Omnivisible stinker*, hailed saviour of Italy" [Onnivisibile fetente salutato salvatore dell'Italia].

Then, with two topazed fingers, she lifts her skirt, "in front, revealing to one and all that she was wearing underwear" [sul davanti, (aveva) palesato a tutti che ciaveva le mutanne] (269/194). The excited rat/topaz, homing, as it were, takes what for it is "the path of duty" [la via del dovere], and climbs up her legs, "fat and trembling with terror, making her laugh…, raving from its tickling" [grasso e nel suo terrore fremente, la faceva ridere…, smaniare dal solletico]. And there, finally, it stops short: "they were made of cardboard and plaster, her underpants, that time" [ce l'aveva di cartone e di gesso, le mutanne, quella volta] (269/194).

* * *

There is no doubt that Pestalozzi's dream is a *mise en abyme*,[121] a subtext of closure, at more than one level: it is the hermeneutic model for the system of gender and subjectivity operative as theme in the novel, and more, it is the hermeneutic model for the generation of narrative.

First, in the dream story there is an actual closing, signifying all the other forms of closing up, or resistance, as I have called it, attribute of the female characters analyzed, with intrusion of male conceptualization as its complement.

In that territory of the dream "where names thin out*" [dove i nomi si diradano]

(266/193), a number of equivalences are established by lexical and semiotic elements in the dream. Other subtexts, belonging to the narratives of these characters are explicated and in turn explicate the dream subtext.

If we reduce the prominent women of the novel to two categories, they are those of mistresses and maids, of teacher and apprentices, of thaumaturge and hierophants: on one side, Liliana and Zamira, on the other the nieces/maids, the nieces/apprentices, the apprentices/nymphs.[122]

To begin at the lower rank, Liliana's maids/nieces (among whom Assunta), Zamira's nieces/apprentices (among whom Ines) and Circe's nymphs are one: big-bosomed and exuding vitality and fertility like the sabellic Assunta, the nymphs/apprentices[123] of the dream, like Ines, "wriggle out" [si divincolavano] from every "twisting/tormenting veto of the fathers" [torquente veto dei padri] (267/193; my translation), and the "prompt erection... both of neck and of head" [subita erezione... e del collo e del capo] signifies "the untamed pride both of the cervix and of the spirit" [la indomita alterezza e della cervice e dell'animo]. Like Ines, they go to the underbrush ("macchia" is used in both subtexts), or, in a Sappho-like gesture, throw themselves into the sea.

Then, through overlapping units of signification, equivalences are set up between Liliana, Zamira, and Menegazzi/Circe. Thus, Zamira and Circe are sorceresses, drunk and disheveled, distilling propitiatory or repellent philters, instilling "a quantum of energy" (Zamira),[124] or a lack of it, as the case may be, in males, manipulating them, that is, like Liliana, like women in general.

More important, the vulgar cleft of Circe's mouth, splitting her face from ear to ear, is a variant of Zamira's toothless mouth, "stretched at the corners into a dark and lascivious smile... and, no doubt involuntarily, coarse" [si stirava agli angoli in un sorriso buio e lascivo... e, certo involontariamente, sguaiato] (200/147), which in turn corresponds to Liliana's wound, and lower, to the "obscenity of that pose" [(l)a turpitudine di quell'atteggiamento] (84/69), with its "parted legs".

Of course, all three, with their literal or symbolic mouths/ vaginas, laugh at male rationality, industry, desire: Zamira at Pestalozzi's attempt to interrogate her pupils, Circe at the soon-to-be-disappointed rat. And Liliana, with her gaping, bubbling, wound, with the exposed red strands of the veins in her throat, perplexes the novice policemen for whom the slashed veins are "curious forms" (69/59), as she ultimately perplexes Ingravallo himself, for all his capacity to identify the carotid, the jugular, for all his (anatomical) knowledge.

The countess of the dream, unlike her nymphs and other maids,[125] she had her underwear. The meaning of this curious protest is located in the use of an index of virginity, an intratextual reminder of the dead Liliana. Contessa Circia raised her skirt "revealing to one and all that she was wearing underwear. She was wearing it, the sainted woman: yes, yes, yes,* she was, she was*" [(aveva) palesato a tutti che ciaveva le mutanne. Ce l'aveva, la santa donna, le mutanne: sì sì sì ce l'aveva ce l'aveva] (269/194). The last quote shows, in addition, the assimilation of the whore Zamira, "la santa donna", to the virginal Madonna Liliana.

On the other hand, the dream's rat (the topaz, the jewel that the countess Menegazzi lacked), shares a common frustration with Zamira's "cautious" rats, coming tiptoeing into her cellar, that "sacellum* or oracular receptacle" [sacello o ricettacolo responsale] (205/150), drawn by an irresistible olfactory attraction, "l'odor di cacio" of a mountain pecorino cheese, the equivalent of Circe's snuffbox. But, "locked and barred" [chius(o) a spranga] (206/152), this object of desire will remain unreachable, forever inaccessible to them, and all they can do is sniff[126] "the Idea, the presence of an invisible Form*" [l'Idea, la presenza d'una Forma invisibile] (205/151). Frustrated in their grotesque cathexis, the rats – and Ingravallo, too[128] – transform impossibility of possession into Theory. An unsatisfactory displacement, accompanied, as we have seen, by fury, madness, fear.

At the end of the novel, the black fold of Assunta's brow paralyzes Ingravallo in a death-dealing, Medusa-like gesture, as at the end of Pestalozzi's dream, when the hapless rat,[128] bound to arrive at his dutiful destination, finds it impenetrable, barred by cardboard and plaster underwear: because finally, "for once, in life, they had put a plaster cast on her* trap" [una volta in vita le avevano ingessato la trappola]!

Plaster underpants block penetration, but so also, conversely, can the open, bleeding, female cavity itself become protection against masculine intrusion. The female "darkness where names thin out" is then the end of the traditional epistemology of closure,[129] in tension with which Gadda writes. In the "endless dream of the night", of the abyss (267/193), resides Zamira's orphic mystery, the unrepresentable female subjectivity.

Second, and more important, the dream subtext, in its position in the novel and by its very nature, is a containable unit. It has a beginning and an end. It is framed. It has closure in the most classic mode. But because it is a dream, its use also allows, like no other narrative technique, the symbolization, at once condensed and hyperbolic, of what Gadda opposes to the classical model of integrity and univocity in writing, which is proliferation. For the most characteristic feature of Gadda's style is that of proliferation: lexical, syntactic, narrative. As dream, this subtext is able to make use of metamorphosis, of the elliptic transformations of dreamwork that facilitate the emergence of the symbolic dimension of the narrative.

One such metamorphosis, indicating the functioning of the narrative process, is that of the topaz (before becoming the phallic rat of the later part of the dream, and serving the theme rather than the form). It is a "strange being", a mad being ("un pazzo"). Then *pazzo* becomes *topazzo* only by prosthesis, but it thus gets closer to the object of the dream, the jewel, the *topazio*.[130] At the level of semantics, the couple *topazzo/topazio* is a paronomasia,[131] but at the semiotic level these words refer to the same being with many facets. The dictionary-like description of the actual jewel, "un vetro sfaccetato" [a faceted glass], with its suggestion of plurality, is too suggestive of Gadda's theorization of reality not to become a sign that the signified will prove to be something different, and more, than the topaz.

A subsequent transformation brings us to the "lamp/reflector", which is, in idiomatic superlative absolute, "giallo giallo", very yellow. The repetition intrinsic to the idiom suits Gadda very well, and announces the textual proliferation, the expansion which follows:

"un fanale giallo giallo, che *ingrossava, ingrandiva* d'attimo in attimo", "a very yellow lamp that *grew, got bigger* from one moment to the next" (italics mine), arriving, a bit later at repetition of its proper name, qualified by "maledetto", damned: "il topazio maledetto". This, by metonymic progression becomes "giallazio", which, apart from the color, would have no translation, or, for that matter, even meaning in Italian. Although etymologically unsustained (the -*zio* is not the same type of suffix as -*ccio*, both by root and stress), on the basis of constant doubling and undoubling of consonants present in numerous instances of phonetic adulterations of the spoken language in the novel (corresponding to dialectal usage), it is possible to read the "giallazio" as the substantivized, and qualified, form of the metonymy: the awful, big yellow thing. This yellow thing is Gadda's detective novel itself, his *giallo*. And Gadda presents us in the dream subtext with the hermeneutic model for his kind of narrative, whose main feature is proliferation: it is his narrative that is a strange, many-faceted being, getting bigger all the time, perhaps malignantly, by way of written magic, progressing in a mad rolling ("rotolata pazza")[132] along the fleeting parallels, the binary tracks (pleasing to the author in their double nature) of the double meaning: female subjectivity and its unrepresentability. And it is this same narrative that then also derails,[133] away from those tracks, into swamp-like, rich indeterminacy, seemingly "interminable",[134] all the way to the dark territory "where names thin out" (193), where words diminish in number and gradually disappear into the silence, the "irreparable denial" that is the end of the novel.[135]

Closure and Nontotalizability

Gadda's technique of proliferation, the masterful plays on words, his erudition, his use of dialects, registers, jokes, shifts and dodges, are narrative devices that serve to increase his authorial control, to produce one controlling voice. Yet, at the same time, it is through proliferation that he seems to attempt to undercut his mastery, to destroy continually the unity of the voice. Thus, since both the device and the counter-device are identical, Gadda cannot escape the bind of writing.

The claim for a nontotalizability in Gadda's text does not necessitate affirmation of any general theory of textual undecidability, indeed, it might seem more at home in a more classical account of closure. It is also the case, however, that this account of Gaddian heterology need not foreclose a reading stressing other ranges of difference.

A mesh of multiple closures traverses Gadda's *Pasticciaccio*, unifying the novel, which yet suggests a nontotalizable plenum of ungrammaticalities, to use a Riffaterrian term.

One wants to say that Gadda's text is all ungrammaticalities, but then, of course, there are multiple connections. If one kept on reading and rereading, could one connect everything up? Such a claim would fall to Derrida's critique of empiricism.[136] But the powerful, though parenthetical, "yet" in Riffaterre's reading of Rimbaud's "Le loup criait" (1980–81: 231) embodies his counterclaim.[137]

Gian Carlo Roscioni offers a very anti-Derridian reading when he suggests that the ungraspable infinite determinations of the world are represented by Gadda's text as chaos (92). Roscioni could be said to claim that Gadda is painting the portrait of an actual infinite, as opposed to a potential infinite.[138] His is an evocative description, but to think of the *Pasticciaccio* as chaos is to create problems in the logic of analysis. Gadda's text calls forth two opposed descriptions: the text has closure and the message of its unities is nontotalizability. This is what Roscioni is describing. The text is nontotalizable, its unities point to their own insufficiencies and excesses.

What is undecidable, at least by me, is whether one of these aspects sublates the other, and which sublates, which is sublated? It appears that to each perspective the other offers its submission. At first this would seem to mean that nontotalizability emerges as dominant interpretation, closure losing by default, because it insists on an end to difference. Difference is no classicist and can always move over. But I believe this fails to account for any cohesion of the text (not that theories of difference do not give their own accounts of cohesion). If difference undoes closure, closure also defines difference.

The quality that works against closure in a text, has been identified by a variety of literary theorists with the feminine/female. The masculine/male is taken as the totalizing impulse to closure. Here it might be possible to identify the pull against closure in Gadda's work as an aspect of this subversive feminine. This would certainly fit with the parallelism between Ingravallo's theorizing and Gadda's representation. I would prefer not to identify the element in Gadda's writing with the feminine, since his text evinces not surrender to, nor panic at, any dissolution of meaning. I don't think that there is any dissolution of meaning in Gadda. Gadda's shame and Gadda's fun would seem to demand a different description.

Need and Theory

Gadda writes of "that pang of daily need that those who feel it are wont to call hunger" [quel morso della occorrenza giornaliera che da chi ne prova si suol chiamare la fame] (303/218). This embodies a quality in Gadda's reading of the world, the fastidious, voluptuous, and distancing irony that reveals with exactitude the brutal acuity of human need. The *Pasticciaccio*, for all its erudite and literary self-reference, is also a study of human need, in "the bestial arena of the earth" [(l)'arena bestiale della terra] (233/169).[139]

Gadda shows the thoughts, dreams, interpretations, sensations, of his characters as elaborations of their various hungers, and his own formation of consciousness, the text of the novel, displays as macrocosm the continuum of theory and need. The novel is a theorization of human need: conceptualization is itself a human need.

Quer pasticciaccio brutto is rich in narratives of need. Lavinia detained by the carabinieri tells herself the story of her sorry dealings with her lover as viewed by an admiring observer. "This happened to the beautiful Lavinia". Her tale unfolds in a series of lonely, interior caresses: "Enea Retalli... had become engaged to the beautiful Lavinia..."

[Retalli Enea… s'era fidanzato alla bellissima Lavina]. In her daydream, she sees Enea giving a ring with a topaz, to her, "to this beautiful Lavinia in a strange moment, as if he were going away: clasping her to him, kissing her furiously on the mouth, on the eyes" [a questa Lavinia bellissima in uno strano momento, come chi parta: stringendola a sé, baciandola furiosamente sulla bocca, sugli occhi] (342/245). She wore the ring in fact at Zamira's, exciting amazement and envy in the other girls.

Something that happened is turned into romance, Lavinia's life is interpreted as story. This fantasy is set in counterpoint by Gadda with what look to be the facts of the case: Pestalozzi, embracing his superior's "few and limpid" [poche e limpide] hypotheses, marshals his reasoning abilities for the reconstruction of the small-time crook's gesture: he may have given the ring to Lavinia (and the rest of the jewels to her cousin, Camilla), but more because it was too hot an item to hold (344/246).

Ines, also, sustains herself by telling herself (and the cops) a proud, if painful, story about Diomede, about his blond beauty, his appeal to women, his occasional, hard and legitimate forms of employment. Her own loyalty to him, her justifications of the way he treated her, are also incorporated into the romance: she had held on to his photograph when he had wanted it back, for it was "a memento of him! of all the love they had felt for each other!" [armeno quer ricordo! de tanto bene che s'ereno voluti] (231/168). She is broken when the power to create a narrative for her own life is diminished by facts that have always been there but which now she is forced to face.

Telling the story of one's life is subjectivity. It is what protects one from humiliation, what one has between one's self and destitution. But it is also a fable, a lie.[140] Yet such lies, such theorization of self remain a medium of access to reality.

The book ends with a scene of destitution: the utter poverty of the home of Assunta where her father lies dying, a poverty thrown into relief by the gifts of "the Signora" Liliana. Ingravallo challenges Assunta about this generosity: " 'Remember the person who helped you so much, when you deserved so little' " [Ricordatevi di chi v'ha tanto aiutato, mentre lo meritavate così poco]. Assunta's response is powerful: "why didn't I deserve it?" [perché nun me lo meritavo?] (387/276). That something that answered her need ought not to have answered it is unintelligible to her.

In semiotic symmetry with her answer, we find Ines telling the policemen (those "underfed males") of the last meal she had before being pulled in. "I was so hungry I couldn't see straight" [Na fame che nun ce vedevo], she begins, "I was so hungry!" [Na fame!]. In Piazza Vittorio, she runs into Diomede's brother Ascanio who is selling his roast pork, and gives her a sandwich.

I told him right out that I was hungry… . He understood me: he had already caught on, the moment he saw me. That was the last food I ate: something to stick to my ribs, before I ended up here. I was lucky!

Je lo dissi chiaro e tonno che ciavevo fame… . Lui mi capì: m'aveva già capito solo a vedemme in faccia. So' l'urtimi bocconi boni che me so' magnato: un po' de sostanza prima de cascà qua. Manco male! (256/185)

Ingravallo philosophizes on an empty stomach (7/17).

The Simple-Minded Sign

Eros and Priapo, published in 1967, could be considered Gadda's gloss to the *Pasticciaccio*. A corpus of diatribes against the male narcissism and female hysteria of the Fascist psyche, it elaborates the sociolinguistic critique operative in the novel.[141]

Violent invectives against Mussolini punctuate the *Pasticciaccio*, their fierce wordplay a rhetoric of furious contempt. No mere tangents, as at first they might seem, Gadda's anti-Fascist invectives bear complex interrelations to all the novel's themes, though to none more than to those of reproduction and language.[142]

In *Eros e Priapo* Gadda writes of the deployment of power of the Fascist theory and pragma ("pragma *coûte que coûte*"), of the proliferation of the laws and ideological myths of Fascism, as verbal inflammation, an "inexhaustible cornucopia", but one that comes out of the "Verbo sterile" [sterile Logos] (1967: 61; translation mine).

One such phenomenon is represented in the novel by the operations of the Touring Club of Italy, headed by the Milanese engineer Luigi Vittorio Bertarelli. He had "sown Italy" [perseminato l'Italia] "with the rare seed" [del seme raro] of peremptory injunctions, or of "their symbols imported from Milan",[143] like: "*Dangerous curve! Railroad crossing! Bumpy road!*" [Svolta pericolosa! Passaggio a livello! Cunetta!] (216/158; italics in the original).[144]

Gadda plays on seed and sign, describing "that desire to erect iron stakes in all of Italy" [quella voglia di rizzar ferri in tutt'Italia], and upon them road signs, in order to "inculcate in the bungling velocipedists*[145] respect for the disciplines of the roadways*…" [inculcare a' veloci-pedastri il rispetto delle discipline viatorie].

The Touring Club president is an addlebrained semiotician. He has a passion for signs, but what signs they are! Taking "as pretexts the most innocuous, the most sleepy crossings, every curve, every bifurcation,* every bump" [a pretesto i più innocui, i più sonnacchiosi livelli, ogni curva, ogni bifurcazione, ogni cunetta], the project's sponsors seek to discipline the motorists' motion, by repeating again and again the same set of standardized injunctions, by repeating the same signs. They theorize the real in minimalist terms. The desire to standardize the demarcation of reality by putting on every little twist in the road the same warning sign, is in absolute contrast to Gadda's own semiosis of every twist of reality, taken up, as it is, with description and specificity.

Gadda groups the road signs with "the totalitario-politico signs", the aphorisms of Mussolini publicly inscribed all over Italy. The desire for unambiguous regulation of reality, that semiotic activity representative of the fascistic state and of male bourgeois industriousness, is repulsive to Gadda. So he makes this literal, reductive proliferation the target of his sarcasm. And the way he illustrates both is by breaking up and repeating, in a series of synecdoches in apposition, the name of the inventor of the road "symbols", with its Milanese versions: "the technical memento of Bertarelli, of Vitòri, of Lüis" [(i)l memento tecnico del Bertarelli, del Vitòri, del Lüis].

The disquisition on the Italian Touring Club is, as noted earlier, a subtext, and an example of Gadda's own kind of proliferation. In it, as throughout his narrative, Gadda's signs oppose those of Bertarelli: there is in Gadda a semiotic undertow, a dimension of sound and symbolism that makes the marking of the multiple crossroads of his semiotics almost impossible.[146]

He uses the anthem itself of this worthy organization to dramatize the contrast. Described as "a nobly caesuraed hymn, like the Marseillaise, and like all anthems in general, with a bold impetuousness in the refrain" [nobilmente cesurato inno, come la Marsigliese e come ogni inno in genere, dall'impeto ardimentoso del refrain], it ends with the line: "Ahead, ahead, away!" [Avanti, avanti via!] (217/159; translation mine). This, Gadda comments, "eliminates, as one can see, any possibility of going backwards*" [esclude, come si vede, ogni possibilità di marcia indietro] (217/159).

Gadda's signs of difference, his text that folds back on itself, the counter-theorizing practice of semiotic proliferation, serve to destroy the possibility of a controlling unity, as likewise they seem to undercut the unity of his own authorial discourse.

"Born Illiterate": Writing and Representation

In another subtext, a small passage of the *Pasticciaccio* recounts the tale of the railroad uncle of one of the "country-side Venuses" [veneri della campagna] (245/177) who populate the second part of the novel. The uncle's role is minimal. It involves a telephone call by means of which he is informed that Camilla, his niece, had been taken to the police station as a witness. Upon receiving this ominous communication, he panics, becomes aphasic. Yet, since "volere è potere", to will means to be able to, he does have a linguistic mastery of sorts. He can read the telegraph tape, and tick the keys in response "like it was nothing at all" [come gnente fosse], even though, says Gadda, "he was born illiterate, like all of us" [era nato analfabeta, come tutti noi] (332/237–8). This observation, like so many in Gadda's text, has no discernible narrative motivation. Moreover, most of the characters in this second section of the novel could be safely said to be illiterate, or almost illiterate, so this is not what gives him specificity. In fact nothing makes him special, except that he provides the occasion for the more significant second part of the sentence: "come tutti noi". Not illiterate like all the other characters, but like all of us, like the author himself. Furthermore, the point here is not merely that the category of being "born illiterate" includes Gadda, but that, having no function in the narrative, this characterization is a self-reflexive commentary on the text, Gadda's own commentary upon his act of writing. It is he, Gadda, this most literate of writers, who was born illiterate.

Born also timid, "vis-à-vis the black vulcanite cup" of the telephone, the uncle emits "cautious monosyllables: and few even of those" [monosillabi guardinghi: e pochi anche di quelli] (ibid.). The uncle is wary, while Gadda, with his "full linguistic usage", risks moral abuse. The uncle speaks in monosyllables (and few of them, for that matter), while Gadda, with his doubles and triples and quadruples (and not few, but many), emits excess, excess of literacy.

The Gaddian text disperses itself even as it evokes the real. Recognizing representation as a species of theorization, and thus of violence, Gadda constructs a narrative whose very richness is its own undoing. His pleasure and his shame remain ineluctably entwined, threads of the practiced knowledge of his writing. Gadda reads his own literacy as no more and no less than Ingravallo's ugly knowing practice, *praticaccia*.

Quer pasticciaccio brutto is no purely philosophical exposition of concepts of causality, for example, or of the deformed and deforming nature of knowledge. It is a narrative practice, a novel about the stories, "the cases of men: and women". Gadda's art itself is *praticaccia* of his so-called Latin world.

Notes

1   Translated into English by William Weaver in 1965 with the title *That Awful Mess on Via Merulana*. The quotations from the English edition will be followed only by the page number. The same method will be used for the original, as published in the most recent collection of all Gadda's works, *Romanzi e racconti*, edited by Dante Isella in 1989. The references will be consolidated in one parenthesis, in the following format: page of English edition/page of Italian edition; other notations (e.g.: 21/18; italics mine). Other works by Gadda will be identified by year of publication and page number. When a reading closer to the Italian original is necessary, an asterisk will indicate that the translation has been modified. Works by other authors will only be shown by name of author and page, or, in the case of authors with several works, by year and page.

2   The word in Italian is *fantasia*, which carries connotations of phantasm/phantom and fantasy, both playing a role in the economy of the novel (see pp. 29, 105–6, 134).

3   "Un romanzo! Con dei personaggi femmine! Con quel po' po' di pratica che Cristo gli aveva fatto fare, tanto che non intorpidisse, della psiche umana! Della psiche! E anche della sua stessa" (1987: 420).

4   Marina Fratnik offers a suggestive reading of difference in Gadda in Saussurian-Jakobsonian terms, rather than through the fracture of representational dualism. But she ties this to a psychological interpretation of Gadda's enterprise with which I strongly disagree; she sees Gaddian verbal proliferation as issuing from frustration in the attempt to find the right word ("le mot prôpre"), which she also calls "illusion" (169). For Fratnik, this frustration does bear on the "ontological" divide between language and reality, but she finds in Gadda (as in his protagonist) a linguistic or conceptual doubt generating lists of equivalent expressions, all equally not good, whereas I find these expressions not equivalent and all equally good, and will argue that the doubts (Gadda's and his protagonist's) are better understood as moral, a description offered by Fratnik only in passing (165).

5   In 1939, during the years of the magazine publication of the *Cognizione del dolore*, that book of agonized immolation of self and mother, Gadda writes about his intention to probe "at any price, breaking the most solemn interdictions, the biopsychic mysteries of feminine organization" (1964: 11).

6   To mention only one instance, his book-length essay *Eros e Priapo*. This, Gadda's most virulent attack on Fascism, analyzes in a heavily Freudian manner its animal-like eroticism and exhibitionism, in explanation of the dynamics between dictator and society.

7   Gian Carlo Roscioni (90–91), in his "empiricist" (as he himself calls it) interpretation, sees in Gadda's exhaustion the reason why his two main novels remain unfinished.

8   As this manuscript was going to press, the very fine study of Albert Sbragia, *Carlo Emilio Gadda and the Modern Macaronic*, which develops concepts and interprets elements of

Gadda's *Pasticciaccio* in ways comparable to mine, was published, but did not come to my attention until after completion of my work.

9   For a discussion of the development of this category of literary history, from Contini, to Pasolini and to the *Gruppo 63*, see Ragusa, 134–35.

10 For a treatment of Gadda's intention to write detective stories, see Merola, 142–45.

11 JoAnn Cannon develops this parallelism, and argues that the *Pasticciaccio*'s withholding of solution causes the novel itself to signify textual space as "detour" (48).

12 All the translations from secondary sources are mine.

13 Insistence on closure in the literary text may be said to find its analogue in the affirmations of classical metaphysics. Gadda's *Pasticciaccio* may be described as an epistemological detective story and this study's exploration of the nature of knowledge and its relation to narrative technique brings to view the continuity between the problematic of closure and that of knowing. Classical metaphysics yields a series of epistemologies of closure, whether this be Plato's grounding of *episteme* in the immutable system of the Good, Descartes' securing of certainty through the clear and distinct idea, or Kant's abolition of ambiguity by his claim for the completeness of the categories (cf. Lucia Lermond, 1983). It is this concern for absolute unification that has come under criticism by the various postmodernisms, as have likewise totalizing theories of textual meaning. (The empiricists have a different place, and have sometimes been treated more sympathetically by postmodernists. For instance, Deleuze has a certain respect for Hume, and also for Spinoza, whom he considers a rationalist with a difference.)

14 I owe these reflections to Lucia Lermond, philosopher and Spinoza scholar. It is Zeno's paradoxes that may be seen to underlie the theory of the infinitesimal.

15 In her chapter, "La disgregazione e il nulla", 101–121.

16 Because of the traditional yellow cover of detective novels in Italy, they have come to be called *gialli*.

17 "Narrative desire" is a category developed in Peter Brook's *Reading for the Plot*.

18 The difference in Italian is only one of stressed vowel, not of an added sound: *patéma* rather than *pàtema*.

19 *Dottore* may refer to Ingravallo's education or to his status, in which case the title would be honorific. It is mostly his subordinates that address him as *dottore*, while persons of the lower class he investigates call him with the regional form *dottò*. Weaver more often than not translates it as "officer". Ingravallo's official title is that of *commissario*, police inspector. The Balduccis call him "Don Ciccio", a term of respect (*Don*, from *Dominus*), but also of intimacy, "Ciccio" being the affectionate diminutive of Francesco.

20 For all his linguistic fastidiousness, Ingravallo mixes two or three dialects (Neapolitan, Molisan, Roman) with Standard Italian.

21 Ingravallo's sexual frustration has something in common with Liliana's tragedy. They share a fundamental/existential lack. Moreover, Ingravallo's perception of Assunta (or Virginia – another of Liliana's wards/maids – or Ines Cionini, who belongs to Zamira's *seraglio*, and with whom Assunta might be considered interchangeable) is influenced by that of Liliana.

22 On woman as Madonna, see De Benedictis, 77 n.17; Sergiacomo remarks on the "absurd sublimation" of motherhood in Fascist times (76). Finally, Fratnik mentions the sonnet in the context of Ingravallo's ties to language and writing (158).

23 cf. Olga Ragusa's essay on Gadda and Pasolini (140), where the point elaborated here is insightfully and succinctly made.

24 In her own right, Liliana Balducci, like the social group to which she belongs, certainly the group of people housed at 219 via Merulana, has reached a higher status. But her social class is that of the bourgeois *nouveau riche*, whose values come under the sign of ostentation and greed ("living... on appetite and phagic sensations" [vivendo... d'appetito e di sensazioni fagiche]).

The word "shark" does not match all the implications of the Italian *pescecane*, which may have the meaning of "parvenu", "nouveau riche". Nonetheless, Weaver had to keep it because the text goes on to develop the metaphor in terms of the sharks' underwater life (22/27–8).

25 Yet, throughout the novel, Ingravallo projects an attractive masculinity. The reader seems to be inducted into his passion.

26 In Molise.

27 Weaver has reversed the translations: in the quote about Giuliano, the Italian verb used is *perseguitare* to persecute, to haunt, while in the one about Diomede, it is *perseguire* to pursue, prosecute.

28 From γαμικοζ, of or for marriage.

29 The Italian word is *misero*, meaning also "poor".

30 Which sublimation itself is a reversal, since Liliana's desire to have a child by another woman (or even by a male, her cousin), is assimilated to male desire.

31 Virgin, as type of the feminine, is also male, intact she is phallic.

32 Guido Lucchini, in a somewhat confusing note, remarks on Gadda's use of the category of sublimation as distinctly Freudian (112, n.5).

33 Valdarena also, earlier in the novel, "brought ladies to his room". Significantly, with the proud approval of *his* landlady (145/110).

34 I am indebted for the discussion of Aristotle to Bruno Blumenfeld, whose translation I have used.

35 The accusation that Ingravallo turns out either banalities or vain elaborations of obscure, crazy (i.e. philosophical) concepts (4–5/16–7), coming at the very first pages of the novel, has a semiotic (in the Riffaterrian usage) function: in the end they prove to be neither. In fact this is a double, or reversed, semiosis, since Ingravallo's deeper knowledge is finally vain, a case of having said "too much" (see last section of this study), but failing to gain access to some sort of closure, some resolution. But such, after all, was Gadda's project.

36 Originally, *gliommero* was the name of a XVth and XVIth centuries' lyrical/playful composition with popular themes, in Neapolitan dialect. It comes from the Latin *glomus, glomeris*, "skein", which also produced in Italian *gomitolo* "ball of thread, skein", and its meaning includes that of "intrigue, imbroglio". *Gnommero* is a Roman version of *gliommero*. Gadda may be playing on the quasi-homophony of this term with the *gnome(n)* of late Latin, "opinion", which itself comes from the Greek *gnomi*, "a means of knowing, opinion, proposition, intent", γνωμη comes from γιγνωσκω, "to learn to know; determine; form a judgement; distinguish". Thus the *gliuommero*, in Ingravallo's deformed pronunciation, is a tangle to be disentangled, to be known.

37 The suffixes *-ccio, -ccia* convey the idea of a bad or ugly quality, as well as of great size or volume.

38 On the prominence of the category of femininity/femaleness, see below, the chapter on Desire and Differentiation. For a discussion of the role played by the feminine in Gadda, see Benedetti, who relates it to his meta-historical analysis of Fascism, both in the novel and in *Eros and Priapo* (especially 92–96); also De Benedictis, 139–68.

39 The term, "fascismo filofiliare", is Bolla's (1976:24). Gadda, in a commentary on his novel, published in the same year as the novel in *L'illustrazione italiana* (now in *Viaggi la morte*), calls that historical period "an age that was avid for progeny" (1958: 114). See also Dombroski 1974: 117f.

40 I have modified Weaver's translation – "...of man's taciturn, final abode" – since the use of the word 'man' obscures the reading that I am developing.

41 One might say that Liliana is the intertext to the discourse of others about her. On the significance of the "privilege of the voice" which belongs to man, from the Duce's own down, see also Andreini, 109.

42   The ambiguity in Assunta's behaviour is itself a sign of resistance. The same is true for prostitute Ines Cionini and Commendatore Angeloni, both casualties of institutionalized scrutiny.

43   Thus is the interdiction "no women" reasserted at the end of the novel.

44   In two different contexts, Andreini addresses the problem of the synoptic view of the author with its parallelism to Ingravallo's in a terminology of the gaze. She says that the detective is "the only eye that sees everybody" and is also Gadda's self-reflection (125).

45   The word *sprovveduta* is, in form, the opposite of *provveduta*, "supplied, endowed, provided". The dictionary translation has it as "artless", Weaver's as "helpless". I prefer "deprived, destitute, lacking".

46   Dante, for example. Gadda, in fact, said in a radio interview, "I would never dare pounce on an unfortunate man, as Dante does, and drag him down by his hairs, in the boiling pitch of rancour and of private revenge". Of course, he is confuting the accusation that he takes his characters from life, when in fact, they are "imagined persons", who "belong to the history of [his] dreams: of [his] nightmares" (1971: 6).

47   Elio Gioanola also develops the idea of the author's sadism which parallels that of Ingravallo's enquiry, but he does so by structuring his reading in classic psychoanalytic terms alien to the orientation of this study (221–22).

48   Pietro Citati writes: "Like Dostoevsky, Gadda takes on the whole moral and fantastic responsibility of the crime. He who tells the story kills, offends, desecrates: is killed: lives immersed in the sacred horror of tragedy" (28–9). The premise of Citati's interpretation is, however, the stereotypical identification of the author with all his characters sequentially, including Liliana's murderer, whose point of view he attributes to Gadda. Moreover, still referring (by name) to Gadda, he notes: "absent-mindedly cruel, his gaze, like that of photographers, takes pleasure in *impious* aestheticism" (ibid.; italics mine), an observation I find distinctly wrong.

49   The verb used is *sdrucire*, "to tear, to rip", as in the description of the torn blouse of Ines Cionini.

50   In Weaver's translation, I believe due to the tortuous syntax, it is the clouds that gather again in unreachable alternation, and thus the phrase "cold shreds of blue" appears as an unexplainable apposition to the clouds.

51   On prolepsis, see Michael Riffaterre (1984). I disagree with Benedetti's point, made in her analysis of the act of representation, that certain elements of the diegesis (among which she cites the clouds), are the "memory of things", empty signs, "presages that foretell nothing", signifying only themselves (120–21).

52   Linking Ines back to Liliana, the verb *presagire* comes early in the book, part of Ingravallo's first encounter with Liliana's secret tragedy: "…those sighs…, those glances that sometimes wandered sadly off… seemed to breach a space or time, unreal, only *sensed* by her… (12/21; italics mine)". The Italian word translated as "sensed" is *presagiti*.

53   Again, Ines and Liliana are linked together by an image of clouds in movement: "Signora Liliana, though with some badly repressed sighs… under the *fleeing clouds* of sadness, was, was a desirable woman: everyone noticed her,* as she walked along the street. At dusk, in that first abandon of the Roman night…" [La signora Liliana pur con qualche sospiro mal rattenuto… sotto le *trasvolanti nubi* di tristezza, era, era una desiderabile donna: tutti ne coglievano l'immagine, per via. All'imbunire, in quel primo abbandono della notte romana…] (19/26; italics mine).

In a letter written on the 14th of May of 1957 to the publisher Livio Garzanti, Gadda, discussing the question of the title, proposes, among others, as a short alternative to *Quer pasticciaccio de via Merulana* (the *brutto* is missing), *Nuvole in fuga*, Clouds in Flight. (Quoted in the notes to the novel written by Giorgio Pinotti, *Romanzi e racconti*, II, 1152.)

54   Weaver's translation of vento *maestro* as "mistral" obscures the issue by suggesting Provence, the region to whose language the word belongs. In fact, the expression does refer specifically

to a northwest wind that strikes also the Italian peninsula. In the text, however, this descriptive detail is not a meteorological one, and so I chose a literal translation, in order to convey the male mastery of the wind against which the oaks struggle.

55 "'Ερος δ' ἐτίναξέ μοι φρένας, ὡς ἄνεμος κὰτ ὄρος δρύσιν ἐμπέτων". Translated by Bruno Blumenfeld.

56 The theorization of intertextuality that has most profoundly and specifically influenced my use of this concept is that of Michael Riffaterre.

57 In a self-portrait, Gadda writes about vengeance as prime mover of his narrative entreprise: "…my story-telling often manifests the resentful tone of the person who speaks while holding back his wrath, his indignation" (Elio Filippo Accrocca, *Ritratti su misura di scrittori italiani*, Venice, 1960, quoted in Ragusa, 138). See also Bruce Merry's study, "The Sound of Revenge in Gadda's Prose". Benedetti, in her treatment of the dissolution of reality, finds Gadda's style to have a double role: that of doing violence to the sign, and that of doing violence to the object (the referent) through the violence to the sign (112–4).

58 In an article on Mauriac ("François Mauriac and Freedom" now in *Literary and Philosophical Essays*), Jean-Paul Sartre makes two relevant observations: first, that "novels are written by men and for men" (23) – whether he means the male, or generically all humanity is, I think, only in part relevant; and second, that "fictional beings have their laws, the most rigorous of which is the following: the novelist may be either their witness or their accomplice, but never both at the same time. The novelist must be either inside or out" (16) (in Todorov, 66).

59 The figures most directly associated with the idea of female/feminine writing are Luce Irigaray, Hélène Cixous, and, in a rather different mode, Julia Kristeva. Each in her own distinctive way 'theorizes' the feminine as a subversive force in language.

60 In Italian, the word for 'lock' is feminine: *serratura*.

61 The connection with Liliana, a 'virtuous' lady, is inescapable, as is the interpretation this apparently unrelated digression puts on Zamira's comment about women as mystery (see p.1 of this study).

62 Weaver's translation is "to cash in", from the bureaucratic usage of *introito*, "cash entries".

63 Most significantly, this disquisition includes Ingravallo's reaction to Liliana's homoerotic tendencies: the entire passage reads: "Ingravallo now was raging with grief, with rancour", whereby Liliana is placed among those he envied and was jealous of (otherwise all male). We might remember, too, that Liliana's gaze, compelling him to transfer his libido from her maid to herself, virtually feminizes him.

64 It is Santarella's gun, not himself, as Weaver's translation would have it, that makes the hearts rejoice.

65 The Italian text, "la maschia boce del buce", is an almost untranslatable word-play, which Weaver renders, with implications absent in the original, as "the male *bouche* of the Douche".

66 At least morphologically in Italian.

67 See below section on Zamira.

68 On the assimilation Liliana-Zamira-Assunta, see also De Benedictis, 156–58.

69 See end section on "Closure and Nontotalizability".

70 At this point, one may say that perhaps the secret of the *Pasticciaccio* is that Ingravallo is homosexual. Critics have developed at length the parallels Gadda/Angeloni, Gadda/Ingravallo. Does this set up an Angeloni/Ingravallo parallel? Stellardi (131), in the company of other critics, presents an argument that looks at both as partial autobiographic 'screens,' with the intention, suggested rather than actualized, of a parallelism. After all, women (as living subjectivity) are ultimately "excluded" from Ingravallo's world. Such parallel makes sense: the whole epistemic economy is homosexual, just as the male writer writes for men. This would fit with accounts of culture/representation as covert male homosexuality, such as Irigaray's or Sedgwick's. For a development of (latent) homosexual dynamics in the novel, see section on

"Homoerotics: Latency and the Failure of the Same".

71 His confusion, during the interrogation, his "sudden pallor" [quel trascolorare] (42/ 41), is perceived by Ingravallo as a *pasticcio*, "trouble, mess", the word later used twice to refer to Liliana's spilled blood.

72 G. Vigolo in a note to Belli, 776 n.6. See also Giorgio Pinotti, 625. Gadda's relation to Belli and the use of dialects vs. language, is a thoroughly covered topic in Gaddian criticism (see, for example, Gelli, Dombroski 1974, Gibellini, Cavallini). Gadda wrote a number of articles about Belli, among which "Arte del Belli" in 1958:161–174, "La battaglia dei topi e delle rane", and "Cantico, cantica, girone", in 1982: 61–79 and 81–91.

73 *Voglia* itself can mean "fancy", "whim".

74 It is obvious that Angeloni shares in the explicit hysteria of Liliana. The treatment of these two characters might suggest that this is Gadda's transformation into story of the Freudian hysteria, which does not differentiate between male and female. Analogously, in terms of narrative development, as Olga Ragusa writes, Angeloni's "preference for food… assumes… the same importance as Signora Balducci's ambiguous attachment to the girls she befriends", both elements being instances of non-linear development (141).

75 Gadda 1958: 115.

76 Andreini's contention that Ingravallo "distances himself from [the canons] of officialdom" (122) is, I believe, only partly true, since his very existence in the novel is owed to the official structures within the framework of which he exercises his function of interrogator, literal and symbolic, as I read the interrogations of Angeloni and Ines. In his definition of the "fundamental theme" of the novel, which he sees as "the danger that individual personality runs when made the object of investigation: justice becomes an impossible objective" in an oppressive society, Dombroski implicitly connects these two tragic figures (1974: 115).

77 In a discussion of his approach to moderation in art ("Come lavoro" in 1958:9-26), Gadda writes: "vanity is not female, it is male" (21).

78 The Italian *doppione* meaning "duplicate, double" and also "doubloon", is used by Gadda as the model for his own coinage of *triploni*, and *quadruploni*.

79 Darby Tench in her 1985 essay offers a critique of a dualistic reading of the *Pasticciaccio*, asserting that in the novel the "process of polarization *turns against itself*" (italics in the original). Here I would affirm her statements on the "duplicity" of duality, but argue that duality is not merely a trap for the "casual reader of Gadda's works", but the initiatory opposition against which every turn twists. Perhaps my interpretation of the novel might be understood as mediating between Carla Benedetti's reflections on representation and irrepresentability in *Una   trappola di parole*, and Tench's criticism of Benedetti's fall into dialectic.

80 Gadda writes that he consciously takes care to avoid "any slippage towards purely narcissistic innovations", but he admits "with horror", that neither his life, nor certainly his "writing is exempted" from narcissistic projections. ("Mi studio di evitare… ogni slittamento verso innovazioni meramente narcisistiche… . Devo… prender nota con orrore che una carica narcisica 'esiste e opera in me': me inconsapevole… Di proiezioni narcisistiche non andò esente la vita. La mia scrittura non ne va esente di certo", in 1958: 21.)

81 On Gadda's 'oral excess,' in relation to naturalism and experimentalism, see Ragusa, 143, and this study's final chapter.

82 In "L'Editore chiede venia del recupero chiamando in causa l'Autore", that served as preface to the 1963 edition of *La cognizione del dolore* (1987: 482). I believe that Gadda's response would tend to undercut interpretation of Gadda as baroque in the technical sense. De Benedictis mistakes the applicability of Gilles Deleuze's category of "le pli" (in *Le pli. Leibniz et le Baroque*) to Gadda.

83 For a discussion about the *distinguo* between characters, and between men and women specifically, and for the modifications introduced in the text of the novel of 1957 in contrast to the

earlier version of the chapters published in *Letteratura* in 1945–46, see Andreini 105–125.

84   If it were Gadda's claim that history is one, this would bear on the issue of an essential monism in his works, but since, as I believe, this is an instance of ironic citation of pseudo-intellectual activity (Pestalozzi's), then we have here precisely a critique of monism.

85   Virginia is the name of a former maid, but also of the latest "niece", a real virgin, *in statu pupillari*.

86   Tench gives a fine reading of the narrative blinds created by Gadda's doubles in the context of Roman mythology.

87   Unless, as Dombroski suggests, we read them as "ironical allusions to the *Aeneid*, loved by Fascists for its idealization of the 'Roman mission' and 'the Latin race' " (1974:124).

88   This establishes the double relation whore/madonna between Zamira and Liliana.

89   With this chicken, Gadda mocks his own concern with representing life: though dead, it "had apparently taken fright and… it had shat, there on Paolillo's little table" [se vede che j'aveva preso paura, forse, e aveva fatto la cacca…, sur tavoluccio de Paolillo] (197/145).

90   In our conversations, Lucia Lermond suggested that this reflection on the nature of representation, is one among many Gaddian Leibniz jokes, here playing on the Identity of Indiscernibles.

91   This "tangle" is the first to be specified in the novel: "Behind that noun 'niece' there must be hidden a whole tangle… of threads, a cobweb of feelings, of the rarest and most…delicate nature. She. He. She, out of respect for him. He, out of regard for her. So she dug up this niece, after years…" [Dietro quel nome 'nipote' ci doveva star nascosto tutto un groviglio…di fili, un ragnatelo di sentimenti, dei più rari,…delicati. Lei. Lui. Lei, pe rispetto a lui. Lui, pe riguardo a lei. Lei allora ha pescato 'a nepote, dopo anni…] (15/23).

92   I am indebted to Luciano Rebay for drawing my attention to the importance of the homosexual 'double' of Ingravallo and Liliana Balducci. His critique of my reading of the *Pasticciaccio* forms the basis of many points made in this section.

93   To be a female homosexual is to act the male. Freud makes them both male; he cannot imagine female homosexuality at all (cf. Irigaray's *Ce Sexe qui n'est pas un* and *Speculum de l'autre femme*).

94   It is remarkable how Italian literary history and criticism has managed, in almost four decades (perhaps only with the exception of Gioanola), to avoid addressing the 'scandal' of Gadda's homosexuality.

95   cf. Rebay, personal communication.

96   An analysis could be undertaken on the relation between painting and writing, suggested by Gadda in this context of urgent desire to create by his use of literary terms: he contends that paintings want to have their say, to narrate (272/196), and the act of painting is called "enunciation" (274/198).

97   An opal, "a stone with two faces", dangled on his belly by Liliana's uncle, "covering" in its movement both the duodenum and the liver, gives him double cancer to the respective organs. Ingravallo thinks that the "double evil eye must come from the bioxide". And to the jewel is related the theme of the double number: "The combined duodenum-liver cancer is one of those double numbers that the cancer lottery rarely comes out with… from the modern cancerological cabala" [Il cancro abbinato duodeno-fegato è degli ambi che più raramente si estraggono . . .dalla moderna cabala cancherologica] (144/109).

98   Death is the decompounding of possibles (84). Is there some sense in which the barren Zamira is yet a creatrix of life? Zamira's mouth is described like a door, from which a snake [of stratagem] issues forth (278/200).

99   This is translated by Weaver as "femme fatale", losing thus something of the Italian meaning, but suggesting on the other hand the connection with fate which I develop.

100   Reading Huysmans as heir to Baudelaire, and especially to the obsessive Zola (of the "heap of pus and blood, a shovelful of putrid flesh" that is Nana's corpse), in fact to a whole body of

Romantic and Naturalistic themes that produce and intersect his work, Bernheimer connects the fear of female sexuality to decomposition and general corruption (378; earlier in de Beauvoir's interpretation of the Oedipus conflict). He notes that Huysmans' fantasy of woman's "swordblades gaping open to expose the bloody depths" (*À rebours*, 1977: 203) suggests that "her sexuality operates a kind of undecidable mixture of male and female attributes" (377). And the "sordid trollop who was laughing in a lewd and mocking manner... her mouth wasted, toothless in front, decayed in back" of *En rade* (1976: 210), is very close to Gadda's portrayal of Zamira.

Rita Felski finds that the subversion of gender norms produced by the movement of the emancipation of women at the end of the nineteenth century, "is a persistent identification of women with vulgarity, corporeality, and the tyranny of nature (1104). There is an underlying misogyny in the subversions of bourgeois male ethos by the antirepresentationalism and antinaturalism of aestheticism (on Gadda and the limits of naturalism, see Barilli). Felski ends her argument by drawing a parallel between the *fin-de-siècle* and our postmodern age in which, she asks, whether it is possible " to detect any similarity between the topos of the feminine in late nineteenth-century modernism and the recent French poststructuralist fascination with woman as a metaphor for subversion – a fascination that is, at least in some instances, accompanied by an explicit disavowal of the vulgar essentialism of feminist thought". Her study, Felski says, "suggests that to dematerialize the natural by insisting on the totalizing claims of the textual may be to echo rather than challenge a long-standing aesthetic tradition that has sought transcendence through a denial and repression of the (female) body" (1104). As for Gadda, it is in fact precisely the dead female body that embodies the most relevant instance of closure (totalizing), no matter how well he may fight closure and totalizability with narrative proliferation.

101 Weaver translates "immemore orgasmo" as "mindless emotion". I thought it better to revert to the perhaps more literal meaning, since the theme of memory is a very powerful one in this novel, one I hope to work on in the future.

102 The closest is General Barbezzo, tenant of the same 219 via Merulana and concierge Sora Manuela. But a mutual interest in liqueurs (and sex?) cannot really be called a relationship.

103 Yet there are impingements. Crime is certainly that. Ingravallo's love for Liliana may falsify and deny her, he parallels her murderer's moves, but in an important sense he can be distinguished. He does not finally destroy her, does not render her actually impossible.

104 In "Literary Language and Every-Day Language" (1958:99)

105 About one of his most important textual features (identified by Contini, 1968:1049), the "maccheronea", macaronic style, Gadda himself writes: "The *maccheronea* is not... the baroque exercise of an eccentric *préciosité*, but desire and joy in the act of portraying beyond the accepted form canonized by jackasses: it is joy in drawing upon the autonomous strata of representation, upon the *practical* spirits of the people... of the souls" ("Fatto personale... o quasi" [Personal Business... or Almost] in 1958:102).

106 The word used in Italian is *imbroglio*, meaning tangle, mess, confusion.

107 cf. also Andreini, 106.

108 An interpretation of the "moldy, yellow, verminous... the stinking, nauseating" gorgonzola (called by Gadda "croconsuelo")--the metaphor for disgust (discussed by Biasin, 34–5) of *La cognizione del dolore* – could be elaborated here, particularly in relation to our imminent remarks on "odor di femmina".

109 In Italian *parvolo*, a latinism, of masculine gender.

110 *Incanalare*, "to channel", is the same verb used for Zamira who 'unkierkegaards' little crooks from the provinces and *channels* them towards working in the city (202/149). Perhaps even this instance might be read as a variation of the role of the feminine in sublimation as we find it in Ingravallo's noble love and in decorous wee-wee.

111 Translating *monte* as "hill", Weaver obviously overlooked the implicit reference to the Latin

mons Veneris.

112 The statues of Dawn and Dusk, in the Florentine Medici chapel, are built on the model of a young man's body, the 'attached' breasts alone signifying femaleness.

113 The word *pignolerie* means more literally, "pedantries", and its etymology may be that of *pinolo*, "pine-seed", i. e. small object, hence equivalent to "cercare il pel nell'uovo", literally "to find the hair in the egg", i.e. to be pedantic, fussy, to split hairs.

114 The weariness of a dissolved unity must be related to the weariness that subjects Ingravallo when theorizing about women, and finally to Gadda's exhaustion. It comes, I think, out of the feeling that dealing with/representing women is an effort that cannot be sustained.

115 At the end of the novel, the exchange with his landlady on the correct pronunciation of the word "anguish" reconfirms the contiguity of Ingravallo's pedantry with his pain.

116 Benedetti remarks on the circular movement of Ingravallo's gaze: from the lower part of the body to the face, from face to the wound and the blood, back again to the face, and again to the lower part, back to the wound and the blood (120).

117 The Riffaterrian definition of the subtext applies to the dream in all its points (1990: 131, also 54–59, 71–77).

118 In Italian the word translated by Weaver as "top-ass" is *topazzo*, and it represents the way the standard Italian *topazio* was pronounced by the low-class "fabulating collectivity" of the neighbourhood on via Merulana. In this particular form, it does not have yet any obscene connotations.

119 The topaz belonged to the countess Menegazzi, resident of 219 via Merulana. Her jewels had become epos "on the stupendous lips" of the women in the neighbourhood, those lips which mispronounced both her name and the word *topazio*. The original substitution (probably on the basis of historical hyper-tuscanisation, as in *piazza – piaccia*) of a dental affricate [ts]), with a palatal affricate ([tʃ]) transforms the name *Menegazzi* into *Menecacci*, or *Menicacci* (with scatological and sexual connotations). Thus also does the *topazio*–topaz become the big ugly rat, the *topaccio*, by hypercorrection, (or, as Gadda puts it, "as a sign of respect"), both in the "story-telling collectivity" [collettività fabulante] and in brigadiere Pestalozzi's dream. There are two other forms used: *topazzio* whose gemination has its model in the centuries-long confusion between single and double consonants characteristic of southern dialects, and *topazzo* as the more economical term (56–7/51). The sound -*z*- is central to the story of Menegazzi and to the dream, with the function of "fetish" (Roscioni, 86). Weaver produced terms like *towpats*, and *top-ass*, which carry only minimally the phallic associations, and not at all the *Nachträglichkeit* of the topaz-rat.

120 Weaver translates *apotropaico* as "exorcizational", while *simulatamente* he misreads as "simultaneously".

121 Gadda gives us a character who quite literally "puts it into the abyss/abîme". Diomede Lanciani, Ines' boyfriend, is given special advice – and attention – by the disgusting Zamira. She takes him into the "cave" [antro], her "sacellum", where he, Diomede Lanciani – mistakenly called by Dottor Fumi, *Lanciere*, the "Lancer" – "bestowed his violent comfort... on the mature dive-keeper,* seamstress and dyeress" [avesse... conceduto suoi conforti irruenti... alla matura bettoliera sarta e tintora] (246/178). Pestalozzi, an *habitué* of that workshop with its "Alban consolations", remembers having seen the young man, "blond as an archangel", coming up on the stairs, "returning from having launched his spear into the Abyss" [di ritorno dall'aver dato lancia in Abisso] (247/ ibid.).

122 After the first interrogation, Ines Cionini goes to sleep in her prison cell, in the company of "other Nereids fished from the ocean by the patrol" (219).

123 The Italian is *torquente*, a latinism, coming from *torquere*, "to twist, whirl violently, distort". This verb is also the origin of the Italian *storcere* used by Gadda to describe the writhing of the oaks in Ines' story. Weaver has it as "austere veto" which does not carry the same force.

124 Zamira services the "dubious", the "insecure": "With ten lire one purchased, through her medicine, the faculty of willing. With another ten, that of being able" (202).

125 Zamira's girls, while beautiful and vital like Liliana's maids, are nevertheless poor and coarse: "What promises, what demographic hopes…! What knees, Madonna! … Stockings--never dreamed of. Underwear? Well!*" [Quali promesse, quali demografiche speranze…! Dei ginocchi, Madonna! … calze, manco sognassele. Mutanne, mbà!] (207/152).

126 The same verb, *annusare*, "to sniff", is used in both rat episodes (205/151).

127 Freud's own footnotes in *Civilization and its Discontents* on human and psychic evolution and the suppression of an eroticism of smell fit here. See Jane Gallop's reading of Freud's "smelly footnotes" in *The Daughter's Seduction* (26–27, 30–31).

128 In idiomatic Italian, the rat/mouse appears in the metaphorical apophthegm "fare la fine del topo" which means "to remain entrapped, or to die without having the possibility of escaping", (cf. *Il nuovo Zingarelli, Vocabolario della lingua Italiana*) of which the dream is the narrative expansion; then the topaz-mouse (*topo*) becomes bigger, and at the end is called a rat, *ratto*, the homonym of rape, from the Latin raptus, of which the most famous example is the stealing/rape of the virgin Proserpina (*raptus virginis*, in Cicero's *Disputationes Tusculanae* 4: 33,71); *raptus* also means "violent rending" in Ovid's *Metamorphoses* 3: 722, and *raptor* had come to mean, from abductor (as in the rape of the sabine women), a robber, a thief. This, coming back to *topo*, is the meaning of expressions like "topo d'alberghi, di treni, etc.", that is a specialized thief, working the hotels, the trains, etc. Moreover, the youth seen fleeing from the building on via Merulana, wears grey overalls, and is described as "un topo in fuga", a fleeing mouse. The mouse/rat/thief/abductor, equates the theft of the jewels with Liliana's murder, the thief with the murderer, and with Ingravallo.

129 On virginal, closed body ("virginal-solid-closed, to be opened with violence"), see Irigaray, *This Sex Which Is Not One*, and Gallop's critique of it in her *Daughter's Seduction*, 80–84.

130 In fact, it is the topaz, *topazzo*, that is the original word, which then, by aphaeresis, becomes mad being, *pazzo*.

131 *Topazzo* is either a phonetic modification of *topaccio*, a pejorative of *topo*, or a mispronunciation (with gemination) of *topazio*. It comes from the name of the Greek island, Topazion, while *topo* (and its derivate, *topaccio*) is traced to the Latin *talpa*, mole. The Latin etymology thus provides the phallic symbolism of the topaz become rat.

132 Fratnik's interpretation of the dream (225–229), referring to the rolling/slippage/ transformation of narrative, correctly and suggestively elaborates the tension of same and other in the linguistic functioning of the passage. She stops short, however, of problems of closure and of the more emphatic and extensive application I give to the *mise en abyme* in relation to gender.

133 On "narrative derailment", see Cannon, 45.

134 In a letter to Silvio Guarnieri of December 30th, 1947, Gadda writes: "I'm still working at my interminable mess, disappointing a little the public who would like to see flow from my pen the river that it cannot convey. I make and remake: mine is a rough struggle, with paper..". Published in *Mercurio*, weekly supplement to the daily *La Repubblica* of November 10, 1990.

135 This expression is used by Gadda to describe another female resistance, that of Camilla, one of Zamira's pupils, discovered holding the stolen jewels. An "hysteric made of stone*" [isterica di sasso], she was "silent, in the silence, outside, of the country, of all the solitary countryside: the personification of an irreparable denial*" (327/235).

136 In "Structure, Sign, and Play in the Discourse of the Human Sciences" (1970:259).

137 For Riffaterre's direct critique of Derrida see his "Syllepsis" (1980†).

138 I owe this suggestion, once again, to Lucia Lermond.

139 Roscioni, in a discussion of Gadda's critique of property, contrasts him with nineteenth century narrative, which had "strong humanitarian character". Gadda, he writes, combines this critique to "his polemic against philanthropy, to his contempt for the 'disinherited.' " The ori-

gin of Roscioni's assertion seems to be the *Cognizione*, in which in fact we do find a bitter diatribe against the "I", the pronoun-louse, and its desire to possess, as well as a no less bitter commentary on the act of giving (referring to the protagonist's mother, which echoes Ingravallo's reflections on Liliana's philanthropy). But Gadda also has a deep sense of injustice. He addressed the issue in many of his writings. One note reads: "When I write my Poetics, whoever will want to understand it will have to go back to the Ethics: in fact, my Poetics will be little more than a chapter of my Ethics: and the latter will derive from Metaphysics" ("Meditazione breve circa il dire e il fare" [Short Meditation on Talking and Doing] in 1958:27). One of his most judicious commentators, Pier Paolo Pasolini, for all his criticism of Gadda's socio-political involvement, or lack thereof, saw nonetheless his moral worth (323–24).

140   Dottor Fumi thinks that Ines is a liar, "tangled up in her own lies" and he wonders "whether she was crazy, or something like it" (223).

141   For the relations perceived by Gadda between Fascism and narcissism, see Dombroski 1984: 110–14.

142   Full analysis of the integration of the anti-Mussolini diatribes in the *Pasticciaccio* would constitute a study in itself. Of particular interest is the positioning of Mussolini at the intersection of birth and excrement (one thinks of Augustine's "between faeces and urine, we are born"). Rome is also so positioned by Gadda, sitting on the egg of her decrees, which drop "at last from her viscera, from the sewer of the decretal labyrinth" (264–65/191). Further, the sexuality/decay theme of Zamira sets Mussolini in parallelism with her. For Mussolini-sex-progeny, see 64–65/56; for Mussolini and excrement, 217 and 220/158 and 160–61.

143   Milan is par excellence locus of technology, engineering, innovation. Ines tells her interrogators that Diomede works as an electrician in order to earn a living, not out of any technical propensity, because "nobody fancies* that kind of job… . Well, maybe the Milanese, everybody knows what they're like: they get a kick out of that stuff: they're all engineers" [na fantasia così nun po vienì a gnisuno… . Li milanesi, be', se sa: quelli ce se diverteno: quelli so' tutti ingegneri] (248/179). Gadda, a Milanese, was himself trained and worked for several years as an engineer. The relation between his scientific training, his philosophical studies and his narrative style has been a critical commonplace (see bibliographical references for Cases, Guglielmi, and Arbasino).

144   All quotations in this section are from 216-17 and 158-59.

145   Not content with ridiculing the automobilist population of Italy by calling it *velocipedista*, "bicycle-riding", Gadda uses a pejorative term, *velocipedastro*, which conveys ineptitude (after all, these are, for Italy, only the pioneering days of motorized perambulation). Weaver renders *velocipedastro* as "velocipederast", which, though irresistible in its Gaddian character, and consistent with the underlying homoeroticism of the novel, introduces to this passage an element unwarranted by the immediate context.

146   This might be an apt description of the work of Gadda's critic, when it does not fall into Bertarelli's folly.

Bibliography

Works by Gadda

Acquainted with Grief. Translated by William Weaver. George Braziller, Inc.: New York, 1969.
Eros e Priapo. Da furore a cenere. Milan: Garzanti, 1967.
I viaggi la morte. Milan: Garzanti, 1958.
Il tempo e le opere: saggi, note e divagazioni. Dante Isella, ed. Milan: Adelphi, 1982.
"Il seccatore". *Paragone* 252 (1971), 3–7.
"Incantagione e paura". *Nuovi Argomenti* 3 (1976), 3–8.
L'Adalgisa. Disegni milanesi. Turin: Einaudi, 1963. (1963*)
La cognizione del dolore. Turin: Einaudi, 1963. Critical edition with commentaries and unpublished
    fragments by Emilio Manzotti. Turin: Einaudi, 1987. (1963)
Le meraviglie d'Italia – Gli anni. Turin: Einaudi, 1964.
Lettere a Gianfranco Contini, a cura del destinatario,1934–1967. Milan: Garzanti, 1988.
Meditazione milanese. Turin: Einaudi, 1974.
Quer pasticciaccio brutto de via Merulana. Milan: Garzanti, 1957. Critical edition in *Romanzi e
    racconti.* Dante Isella, ed., vol. II. Milan: Garzanti, 1989.
Racconto italiano di ignoto del novecento: cahier d'études. Dante Isella, ed. Turin: Einaudi, 1983.
That Awful Mess on Via Merulana. Translated by William Weaver. Introduction by Italo Calvino.
    George Braziller, Inc.: New York, 1965.

Other Sources

Andreini, Alba. *Studi e testi gaddiani.* Palermo: Sellerio, 1988.
Arbasino, Alberto. "L'ingegnere e i poeti. Colloquio con C.E. Gadda". *Sessanta proposizioni.*
    Milan: Feltrinelli, 1971, 94-104.
—. "L'ingegnere e il Manzoni". *Sessanta proposizioni.* Milan: Feltrinelli, 1971, 185-210
Barilli, Renato. "Gadda e la fine del naturalismo". *La barriera del naturalismo.* Milan:
    Mursia:1964.
Barthes, Roland. *The Rustle of Language.* New York: Farrar, Strauss and Giroux, 1986.
Belli, Giuseppe Gioachino. *I sonetti.* G. Vigolo, ed. Milan: Mondadori, 1958.
Benedetti, Carla. *Una trappola di parole: lettura del Pasticciaccio.* Pisa: ETS, 1980.
Benveniste, Émile. "Structure de la langue et structure de la société". *Linguaggi nella società e nella
    tecnica.* Milan: Comunità, 1970.
Bettini, Filippo, ed. *L'alternativa letteraria del '900: Gadda.* Rome: Savelli, 1975.

Biasin, Gian Paolo. "La cornucopia del mondo". *Forum Italicum*, 23:1–2 (1989), 30–50.

Bolla, Elisabetta. *Come leggere Quer pasticciaccio brutto de via Merulana di Carlo Emilio Gadda*. Milan: Mursia, 1976.

Butler, Judith. *Gender Trouble: Feminism and the Subversion of Identity*. New York: Routledge, Chapman and Hall, Inc., 1990.

Cane, Eleonora. *Il discorso indiretto libero nella narrativa italiana del Novecento*. Rome: Silva, 1969.

Cannon, JoAnn. "The Reader as Detective: Notes on Gadda's Pasticciaccio". *Modern Language Studies* 3 (1980), 41–50.

Cases, Cesare. "Un ingegnere de letteratura". *Mondo Operaio* 5 (1958), 12–16.

Cavallini, Giorgio. *Lingua e dialetto in Gadda*. Florence: G. D'Anna, 1977.

Céline, Louis-Ferdinand. *Death on the Instalment Plan*. Trans. Ralph Manheim. New York: New Directions, 1966.

Citati, Pietro. "Il male invisibile". *Il té del cappellaio matto*. Milan: Mondadori, 1972.

Cixous, Hélène. "The Laugh of the Medusa". Trans. Keith Cohen and Paula Cohen. *New French Feminisms: An Anthology*. Elaine Marks and Isabelle de Courtivron, eds. Amherst: University of Massachusetts Press, 1980.

Contini, Gianfranco. *Introduction. La cognizione del dolore*. By Carlo Emilio Gadda. Turin: Einaudi, 1963.

—. *Letteratura dell'Italia unita (1860–1968)*. Florence: Sansoni, 1968, 1049-50.

—. *Varianta ed altra linguistica*. Turin: Einaudi, 1970.

—. *Quarant'anni d'amicizia: scritti su C.E. Gadda*. Turin: Einaudi, 1988. (1988)

—. *Ultimi esercizî ed elzeviri*. Turin: Einaudi, 1988. (1988a)

Culler, Jonathan. *Framing the Sign*. Norman and London: University of Oklahoma Press, 1988.

De Beauvoir, Simone. *The Second Sex*. 1952. New York: Vintage Books, 1974.

De Benedictis, Maurizio. *La piega nera. Groviglio stilistico ed enigma della femminilità in C. E. Gadda*. N.p.: De Rubeis, 1991.

Deleuze, Gilles. *Le Pli. Leibnitz et le baroque*. Paris: Minuit, 1988.

Derrida, Jacques. "Structure, Sign, and Play in the Discourse of the Human Sciences". *The Structuralist Controversy: The Languages of Criticism and the Sciences of Man*. Richard Macksey and Eugenio Donato, eds. Baltimore: Johns Hopkins University Press, 1970.

—. *Of Grammatology*. Trans. Gayatri Spivak. Baltimore: Johns Hopkins University Press, 1974.

"Dizionario del gergo della malavita italiana". *Il Delatore* 2 (1964).

Dombroski, Robert S. *Introduzione allo studio di Carlo E. Gadda*. Florence: Valecchi, 1974. (1974)

—. "Gadda: fascismo e psicanalisi". *L'esistenza ubbidiente. Letterati italiani sotto il fascismo*. Naples: Guida, 1984. (1984)

Evans, Martha Noel. "Hysteria and the Seduction Theory". *Seduction and Theory: Readings of Gender, Representation, and Rhetoric*. Dianna Hunter, ed. Urbana & Chicago: Univ. of Illinois Press, 1989, 73–86.

Felman, Shoshana. "The Lesson of Paul de Man". *Yale French Studies* 69 (1985).

Felski, Rita. "The Counter Discourse of the Feminine in Three Texts by Wilde, Huysmans, and Sacher-Masoch". *PMLA* 106 (1991), 1094–1105.

Ferrero, Ernesto. *Invito alla lettura di C.E. Gadda*. Milan: Mursia, 1972.

Fratnik, Marina. *L'Écriture détournée: essai sur le texte narratif de C.E. Gadda*. Turin: Albert Meunier, 1990.

Freud, Sigmund. *Civilization and its Discontents*. Translated by James Strachey. W. W. Norton and Company: New York, 1961.

Gadda: Progettualità e scrittura. Marcello Carlino, Aldo Mastropasqua, and Francesco Muzzioli, eds. Rome: Riuniti, 1987.

Gallop, Jane. *The Daughter's Seduction: Feminism and Psychoanalysis*. Ithaca: Cornell University

Press, 1982.

Gallop, Jane. *Thinking through the Body.* New York: Columbia University Press, 1988.

Gelli, Pietro. "Sul lessico di Gadda". *Paragone*, XX:230 (1969).

Genette, Gérard. *Figures III.* Paris: Seuil, 1972.

Gibellini, Pietro. "Romanesco e ottica narrativa nel Pasticciaccio di Gadda". *Paragone* 308 (1975), 75–92.

Gioanola, Elio. *L'uomo dei topazi: interpretazione psicanalitica dell'opera di C. E. Gadda.* 1977. Milano: Librex, 1987.

Grassi, Letizia. "L'aspetto figurale-simbolico e la polifonia dei linguaggi nella *Cognizione del dolore* di C. E. Gadda". *Lingua e Stile* 2 (1989), 245–64.

Grignani, Maria-Antonietta and Flavia Ravazzoli. "Tragitti gaddiani". *Autografo* 1(1984), 15–33.

Guglielmi, Angelo. "L'officina di C. E. Gadda". *Vero e falso.* Milan: Feltrinelli, 1968, 56–58.

Hilfer, Anthony Channell. *The Crime Novel: a Deviant Genre.* Austin: University of Texas Press, 1990.

Huyssen, Andreas. *After the Great Divide: Modernism, Mass Culture, and Postmodernism.* Bloomington, Indiana: Indiana University Press, 1986.

Irigaray, Luce. *This Sex which Is Not One.* Trans. Catherine Porter and Carolyn Burke. Ithaca: Cornell University Press, 1985.

—. *Speculum de l'autre femme.* Paris: Editions de Minuit, 1977

Iser, Wolfgang. "Indeterminacy and the Reader's Response in Prose Fiction". *Aspects of Narrative.* J.Hillis Miller, ed. New York: Columbia University Press, 1971.

Kofman, Sarah. *The Enigma of Woman in Freud's Writings.* Ithaca: Cornell University Press, 1980.

Kristeva, Julia. *Desire in Language: A Semiotic Approach to Literature and Art.* New York: Columbia University Press, 1980.

—. *Powers of Horror.* Trans. Leon Roudiez. New York: Columbia University Press, 1982.

—. "La femme, ce n'est jamais ça". *Tel Quel* 59.3 (1974): 19–24.

La critica e Gadda. Giorgio Patrizi, ed. Bologna: Cappelli, 1975.

Lermond, Lucia. "Certainty and Knowledge of the Real in Plato, Descartes, Spinoza, Kant and Wittgenstein". Unpublished essay, 1983.

—. *The Form of Man: Human Essence in Spinoza's Ethic.* Studies in Intellectual History Series 11. Leiden: E.J. Brill, 1988.

L'espressivismo linguistico nella letteratura italiana. Atti dei Convegni Lincei 71. Rome: Accademia nazionale dei Lincei, 1985.

Lucchini, Guido. *L'istinto della combinazione: le origini del romanzo in Carlo Emilio Gadda.* Florence: La Nuova Italia, 1988.

Kermode, Frank. *The Sense of an Ending.* New York: Oxford University Press, 1966.

Maraini, Dacia. "Carlo Emilio Gadda come uomo". *Prisma* 5 (1965):14-19.

Marrese, Maria. "Una fonte per Zamira: nota al *Pasticciaccio*". *Studi italiani* 2 (1989), 115–24.

Merola, Nicola. *La lettura come artificio.* Naples: Liguori, 1984.

Merry, Bruce. "The Sound of Revenge in Gadda's Prose". *Romance Quarterly* 36 (1989), 471–84.

Millett, Kate. *Sexual Politics 1970.* New York: Avon Press, 1971.

Pasolini, Pier Paolo. "Sul discorso indiretto libero". *Paragone* 184 (1965).

Pinotti, Giorgio. "Dal primo al secondo *Pasticciaccio*: La revisione del romanesco". *Studi di letteratura italiana offerti a Dante Isella.* Naples: Guida, 1983, 615–640.

Porter, Dennis, *The Pursuit of Crime: Art and Ideology in Detective Fiction.* New Haven: Yale University Press, 1981.

Ragusa, Olga. "Gadda, Pasolini, and Experimentalism". *Narrative and Drama: Essays in Modern Italian Literature from Verga to Pasolini.* The Hague and Paris: Mouton, 1976, 134–154.

Riffaterre, Michael. Semiotics of Poetry. Bloomington and London: Indiana University Press, 1978.

—. "Interpretation and Undecidability". *New Literary History* XII (1980–81), 227–42. (1980)

—. "Syllepsis". *Critical Inquiry* 6:4 (1980), 625–638. (1980†)

—. "Hermeneutic Models". *Poetics Today* 4:1 (1983), 7–16. (1983)

—. *Text Production*. New York: Columbia University Press, 1983. (1983†)

—. "The Making of the Text". *Identity of the Literary Text*. Mario Valdés and Owen Miller eds. Toronto: University of Toronto Press, 1985, 54–70.

—. *Fictional Truth*. Baltimore and London: The Johns Hopkins University Press, 1990.

Risset, Jacqueline. "C.E. Gadda ou la philosophie à l'envers". *Critique* 282 (1970).

Rinaldi, Rinaldo. *La paralisi e lo spostamento: lettura de 'La cognizione del dolore'*. Livorno: Bastogi, 1977.

Roman, Andreia. "Il *Pasticciaccio* ovvero il fallimento di Orfeo". *Studi Novecenteschi* XIII, 32 (1986).

Roscioni, Gian Carlo. *La disarmonia prestabilita: studio su Gadda*. Turin: Einaudi, 1969. Reprint edition 1975.

Rubin, Gayle. "The Traffic in Women". *Feminist Frameworks*. Alison M. Jaggar and Paula S. Rothenberg, eds. 2 ed. New York: McGraw Hill, 1984.

Sappho and the Greek Lyric Poets. Translated and annotated by Willis Barnstone. New York: Schocken Books, 284.

Sbragia, Albert. *Carol Emilio Gadda and the Modern Macaronic*. Gainesville: University Press of Florida, 1996.

Schor, Naomi. *Breaking the Chain: Women, Theory, and French Realist Fiction*. New York: Columbia University Press, 1985.

—. *Reading in Detail: Aesthetics and the Feminine*. New York and London: Routledge, Chapman & Hall, 1989.

Sedgwick, Eve Kosofsky. *Between Men: English Literature and Male Homosexual Desire*. New York: Columbia University Press, 1985.

Seduction and Theory: Readings of Gender, Representation, and Rhetoric. Diana Hunter, ed. Urbana and Chicago: University of Illinois Press, 1989.

Segre, Cesare. *Semiotica filologica: Testo e modelli culturali*. Turin: Einaudi, 1979.

—. "Polemica linguistica ed espressionismo dialettale nella letteratura italiana". *Lingua stile e società*. Milan: Feltrinelli, 1963.

Sergiacomo, Lucilla. *Le donne dell'ingegnere. Serve, signorine, madri e antimadri nella narrative di Carlo Emilio Gadda*. Pescara: Medium, 1988.

Seroni, Adriano. *Gadda*. Florence: La nuova Italia, 1973.

Speaking of Gender. Elaine Showalter, ed. New York and London: Routledge, Chapman & Hall, 1989.

Stellardi, Giuseppe. "Casi, cause e concause: il 'groviglio' psicologico, etico e gnoseologico del *Pasticciaccio* gaddiano". *Studi e problemi di critica testuale* 41 (1990), 127–137.

Stragà, Antonio. "La scrittura del disordine: esperienza e sistema in Carlo Emilio Gadda". *Lingua e Stile* 1 (1990), 85–101.

Tani, Stefano. *The Doomed Detective: The Contribution of the Detective Novel to Postmodern American and Italian Fiction*. Carbondale: Southern Illinois University Press, 1984.

Tench, Darby. "Quel Nome Storia: Naming and History in Gadda's *Pasticciaccio*". *Stanford Italian Review* V:2 (1985), 205–17.

The (M)Other Tongue: Essays in Feminist Psychoanalytic Interpretation. Shirley Nelson Garner, Claire Kahane and Madelon Sprengnether, eds. Ithaca: Cornell University Press, 1985.

Todorov, Tzvetan. *The Poetics of Prose*. Ithaca: Cornell University Press, 1981.

Wittig, Monique. "The Mark of Gender". *The Poetics of Gender*. Nancy K. Miller, ed. New York: Columbia University Press, 1986.